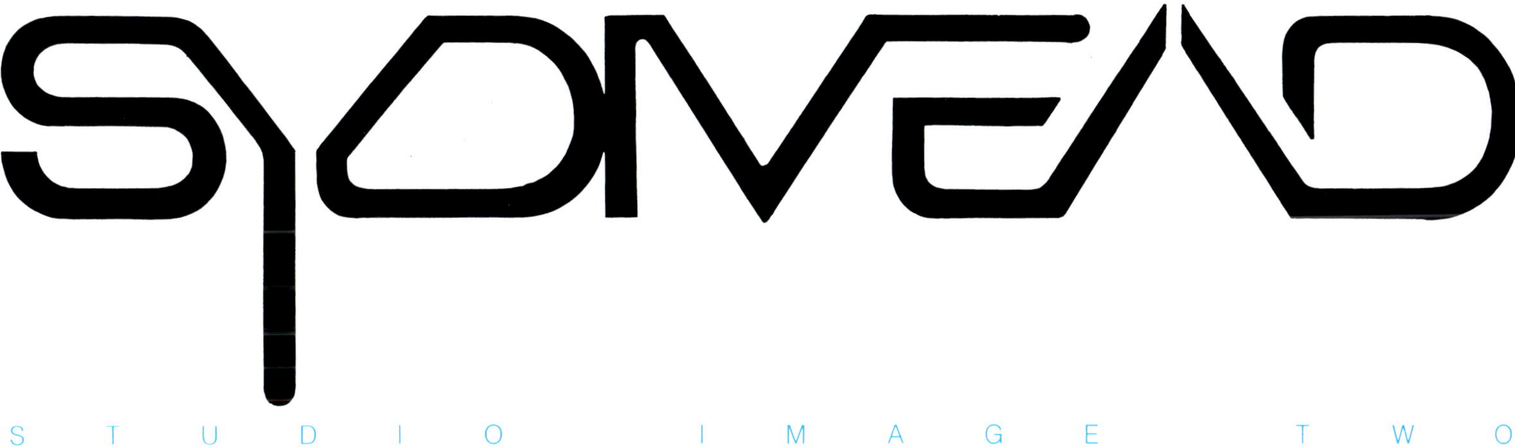

S T U D I O   I M A G E   T W O

In my work I have attempted to convey the technological potential of our age. My professional career has taken me through many design disciplines, all of which have provided challenges in my efforts to find new ways of improving all the approaches. My methodology can be explained as an eighty percent guess of what will be. From this hypothesis I piece together logical scenarios within the confines of the current state of the art. My goal is to encourage the growth of technology and elevate its use.

SYD MEAD

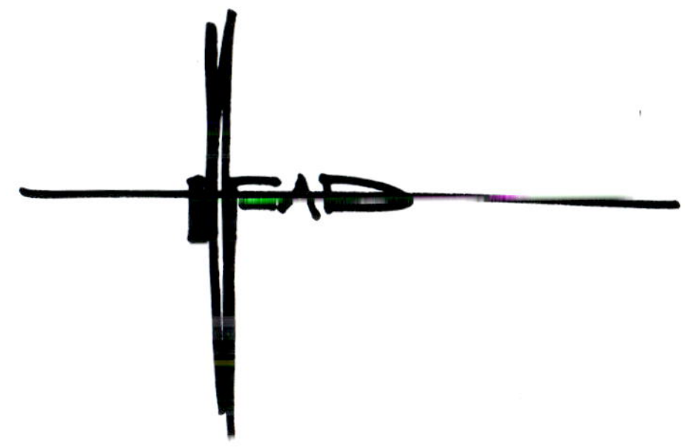

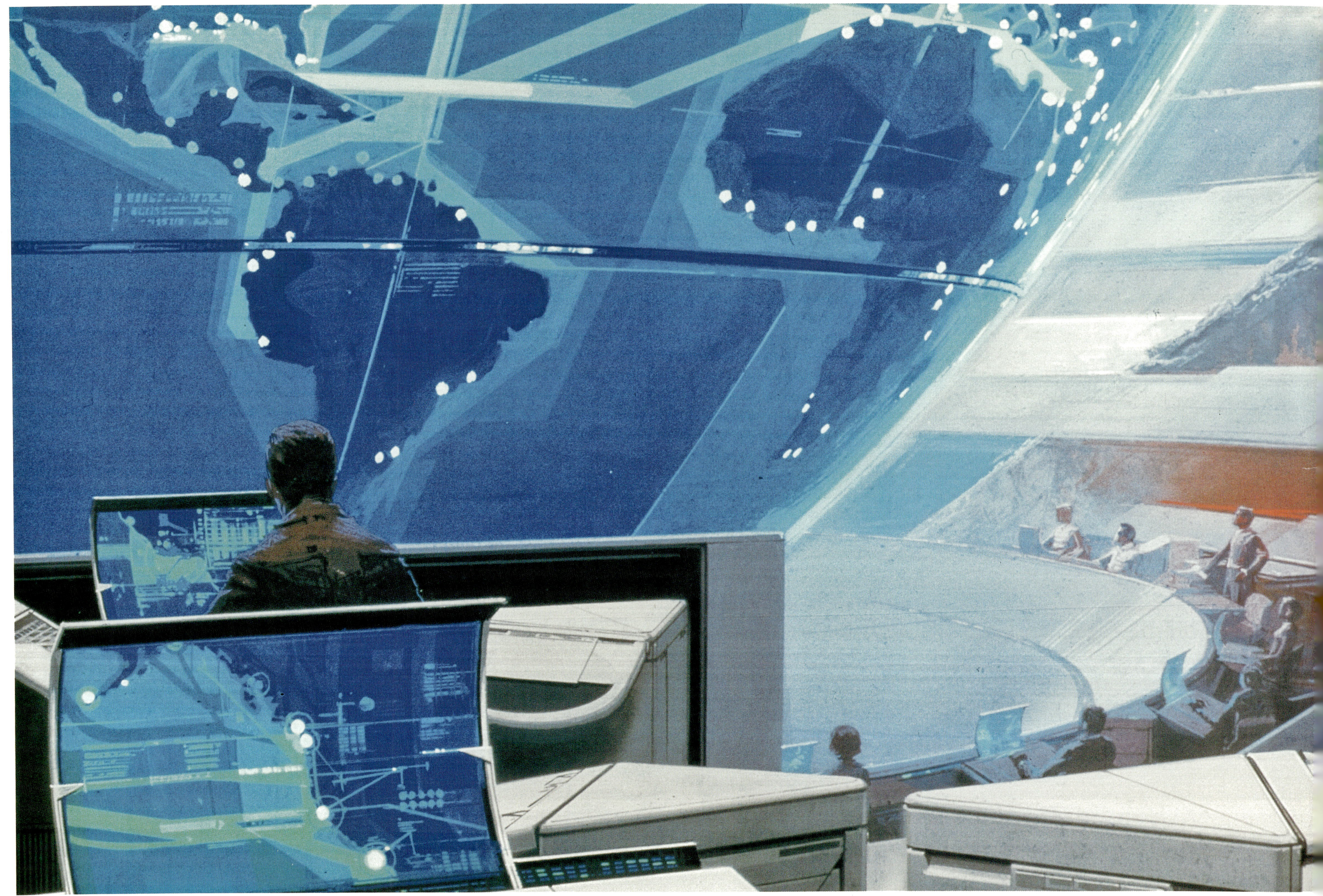

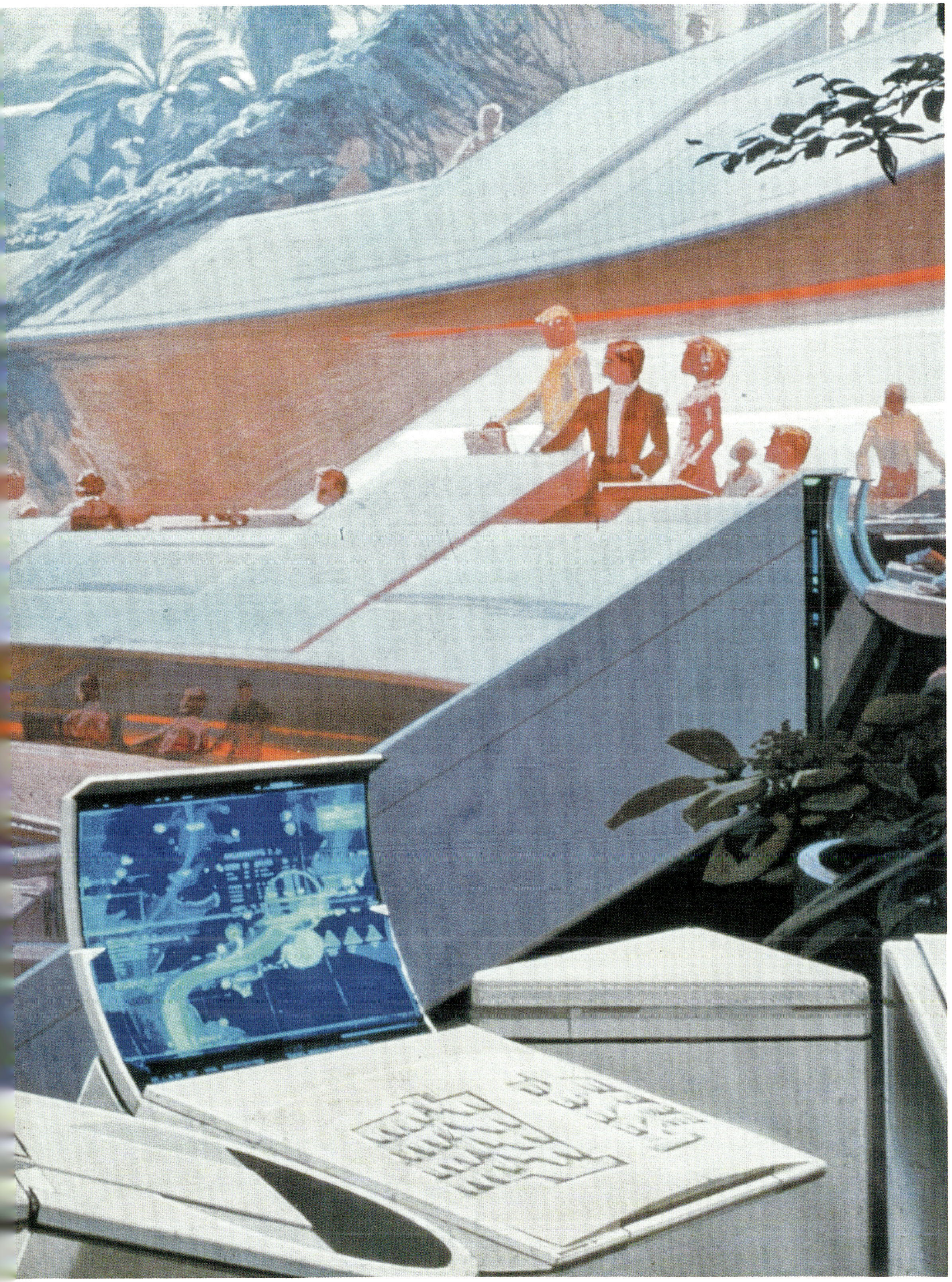

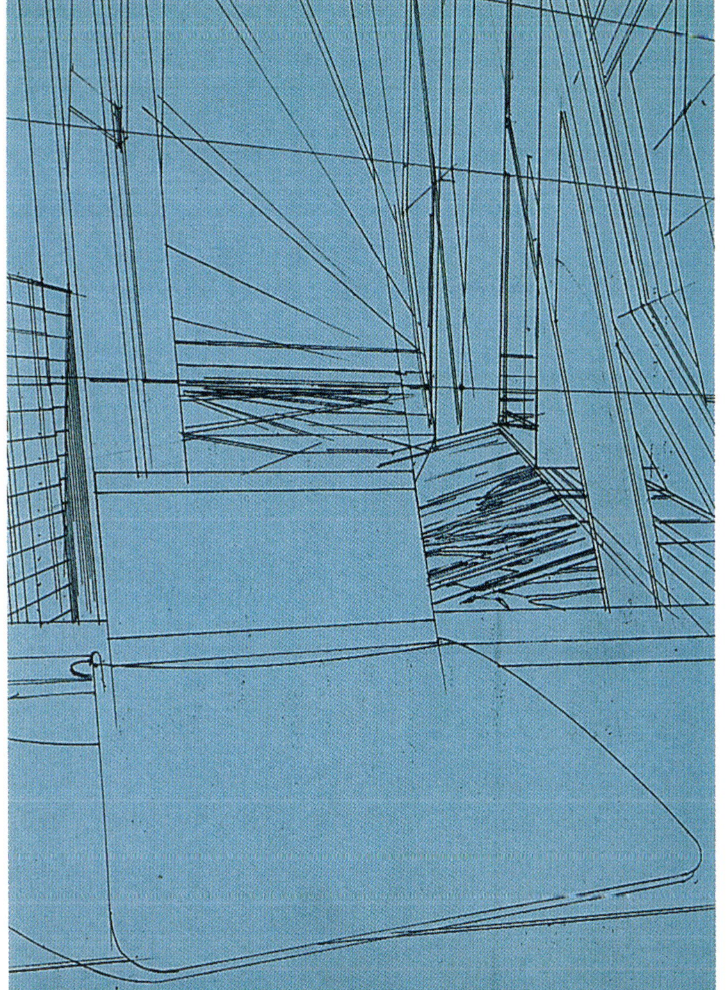
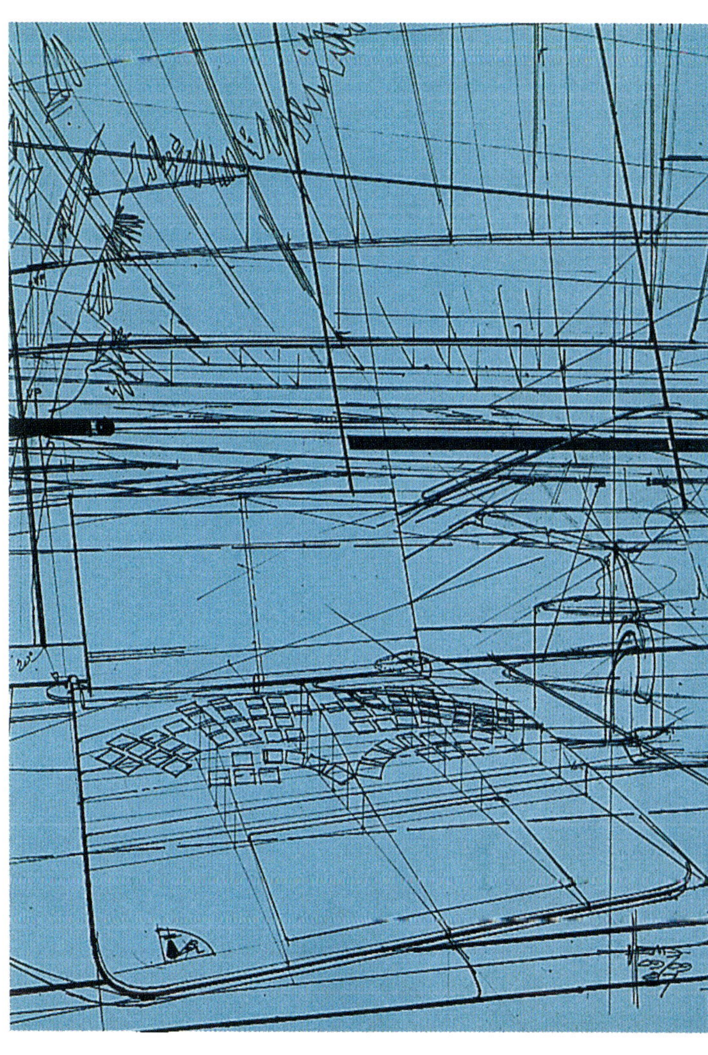
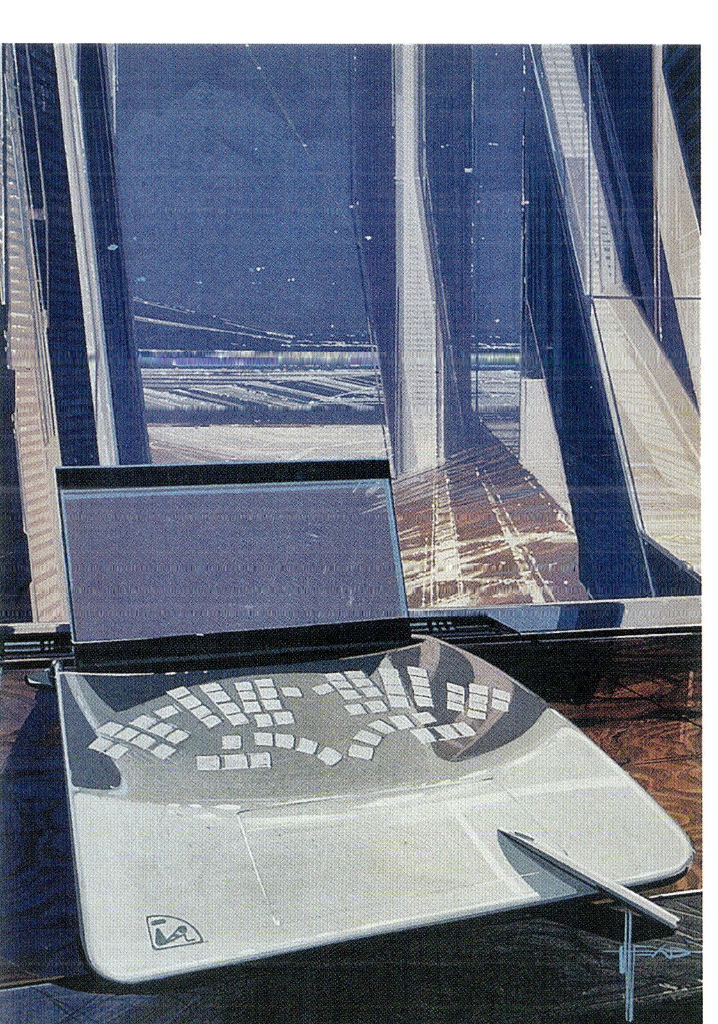
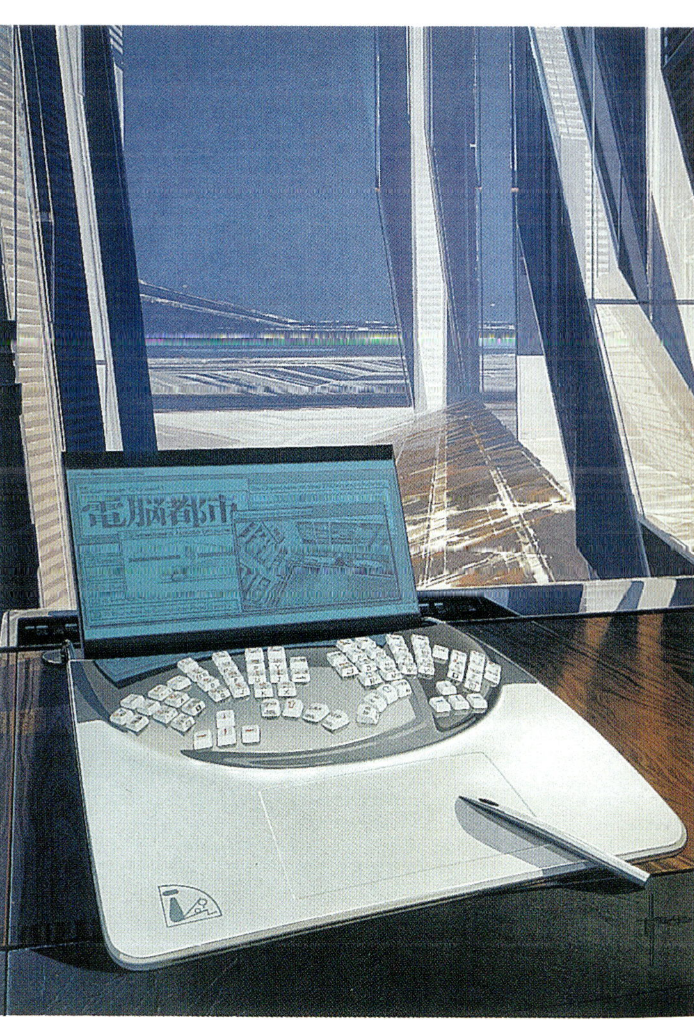

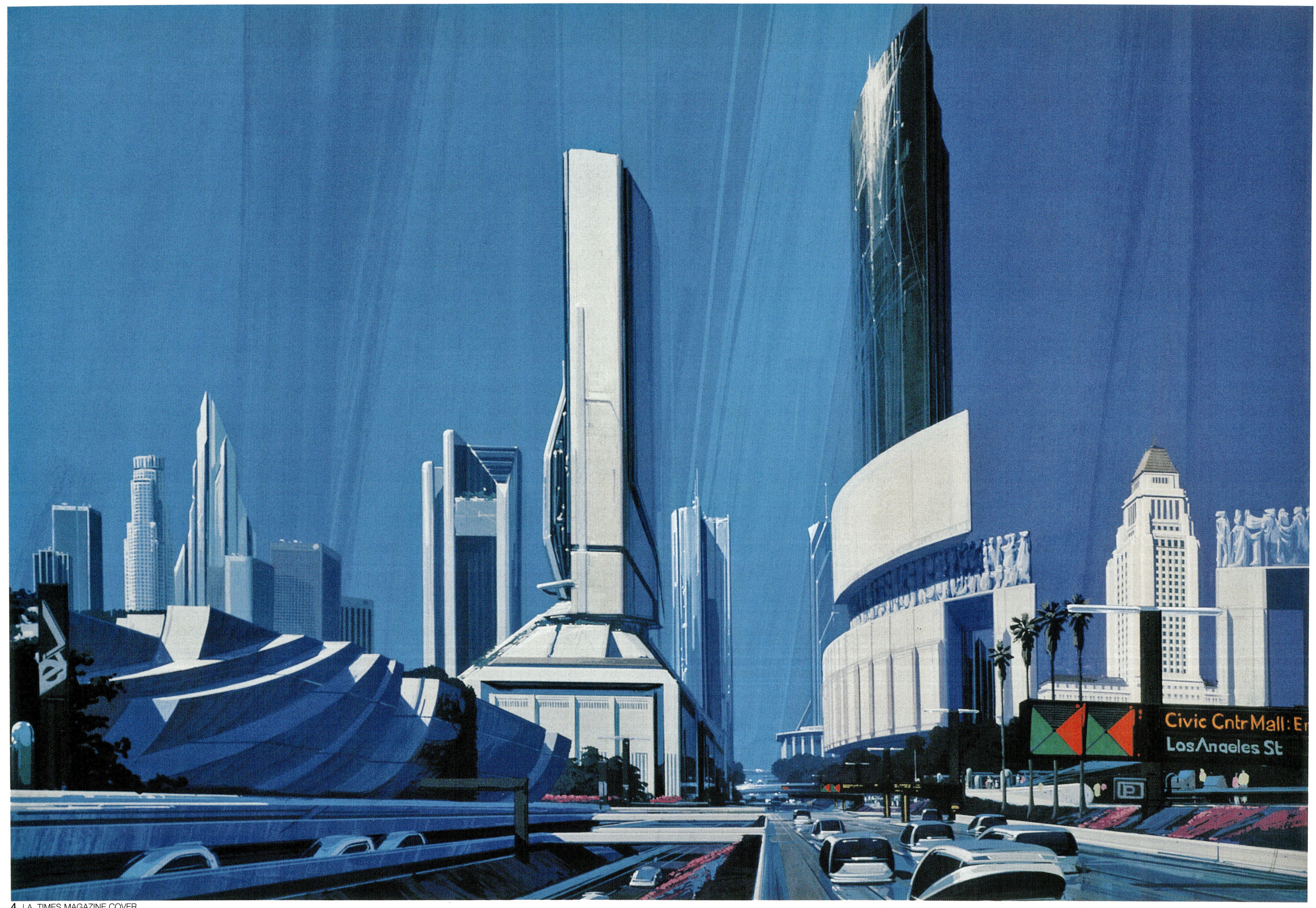

Civic Cntr Mall: En
Los Angeles St

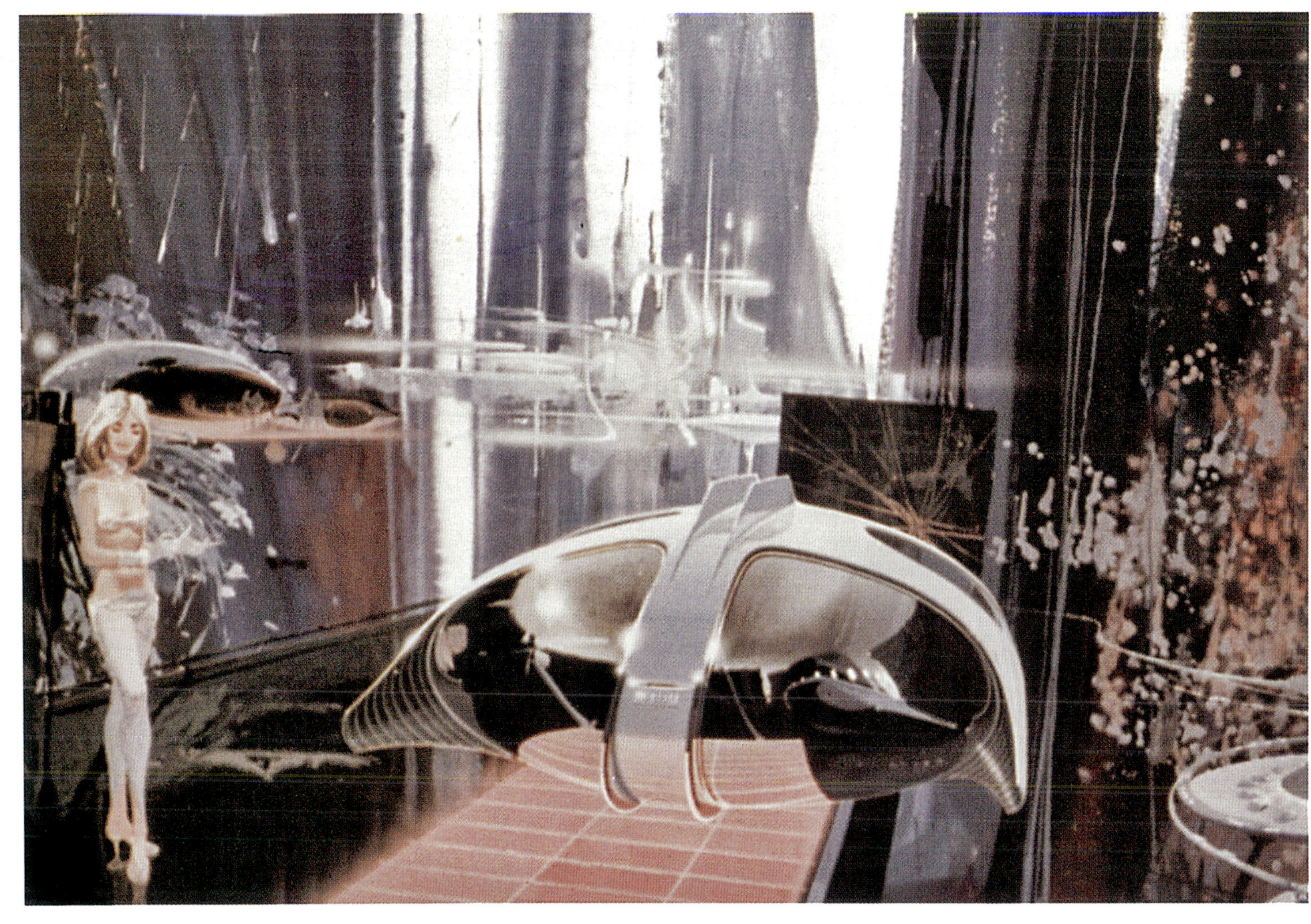
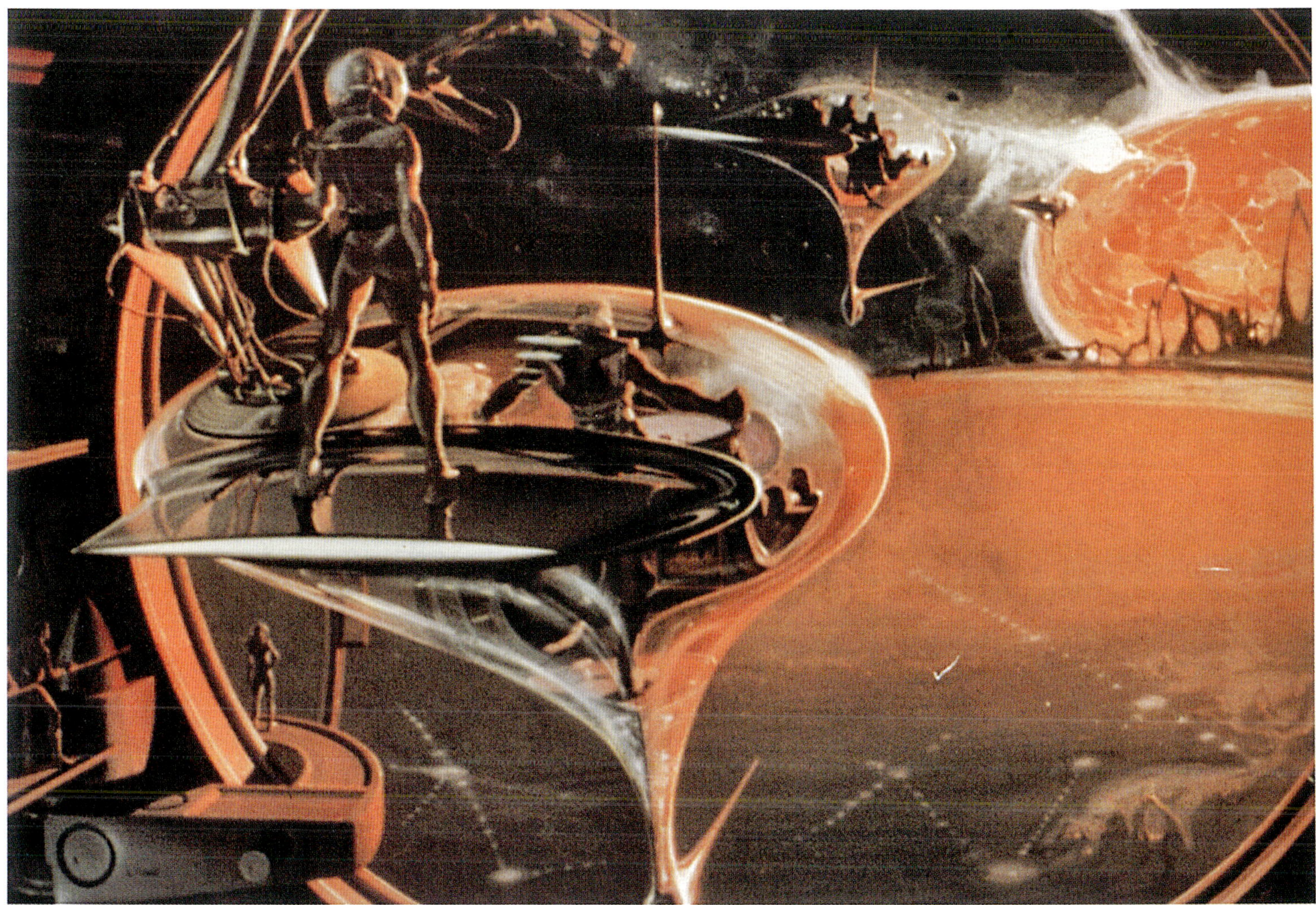
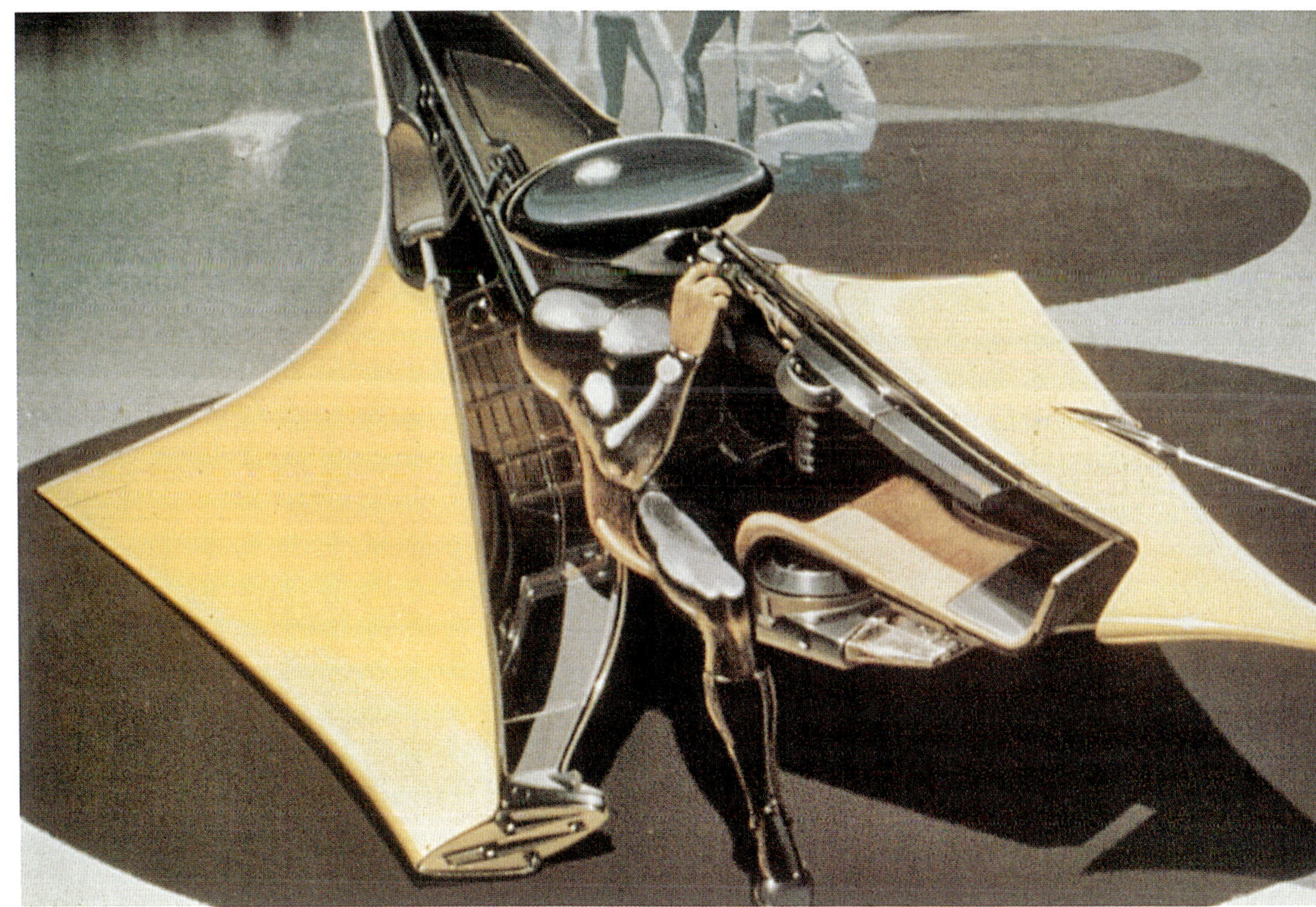
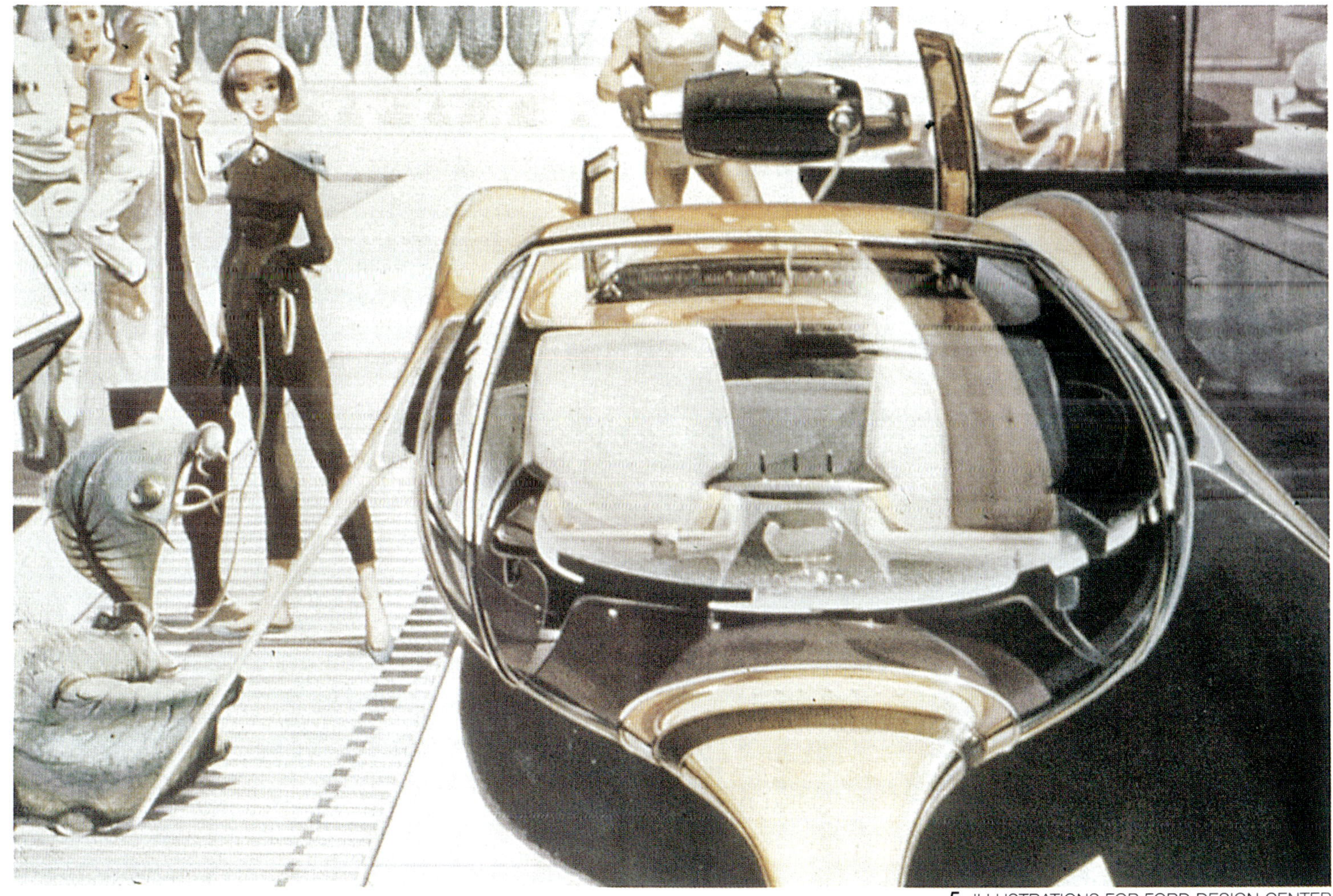

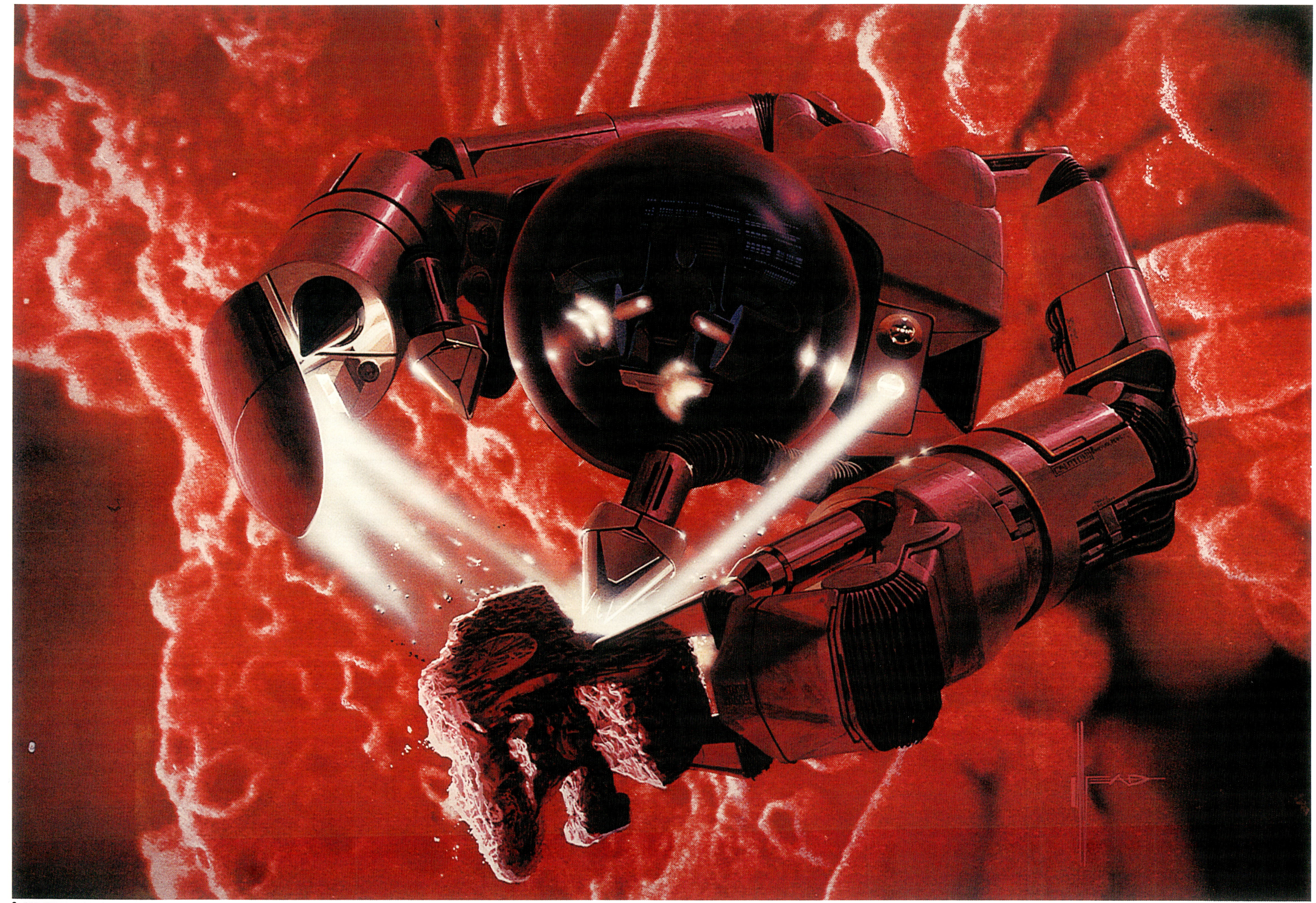

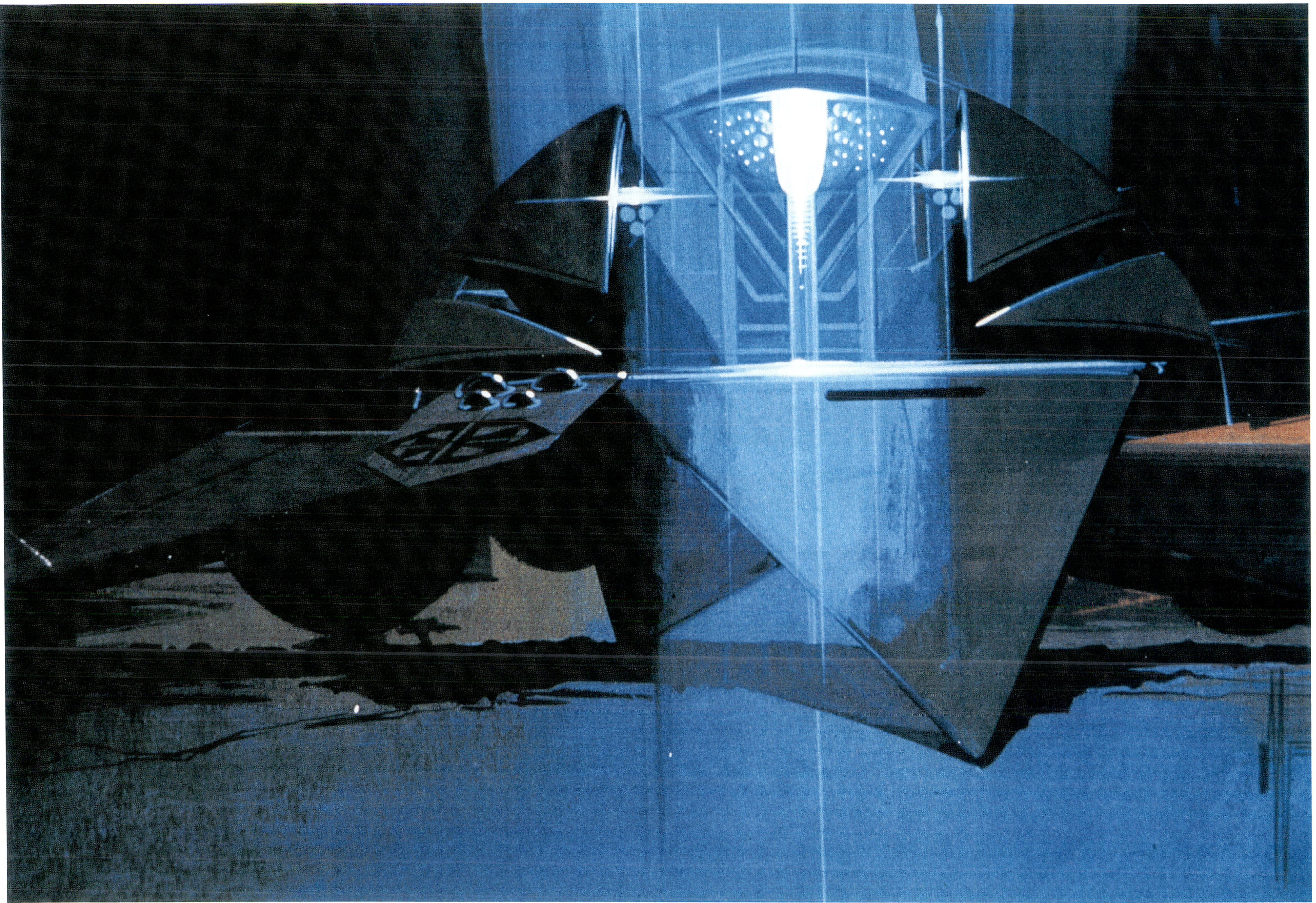

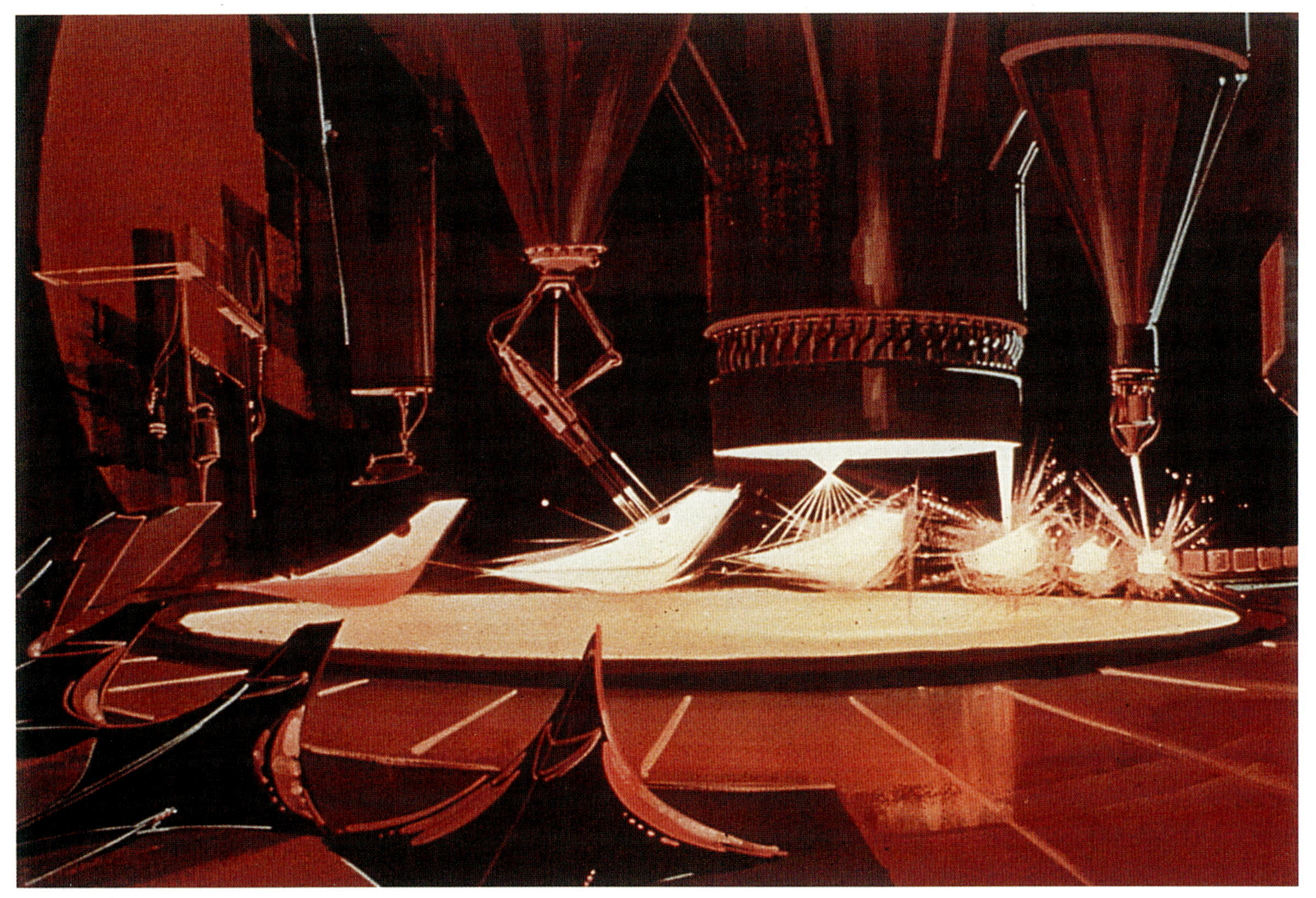

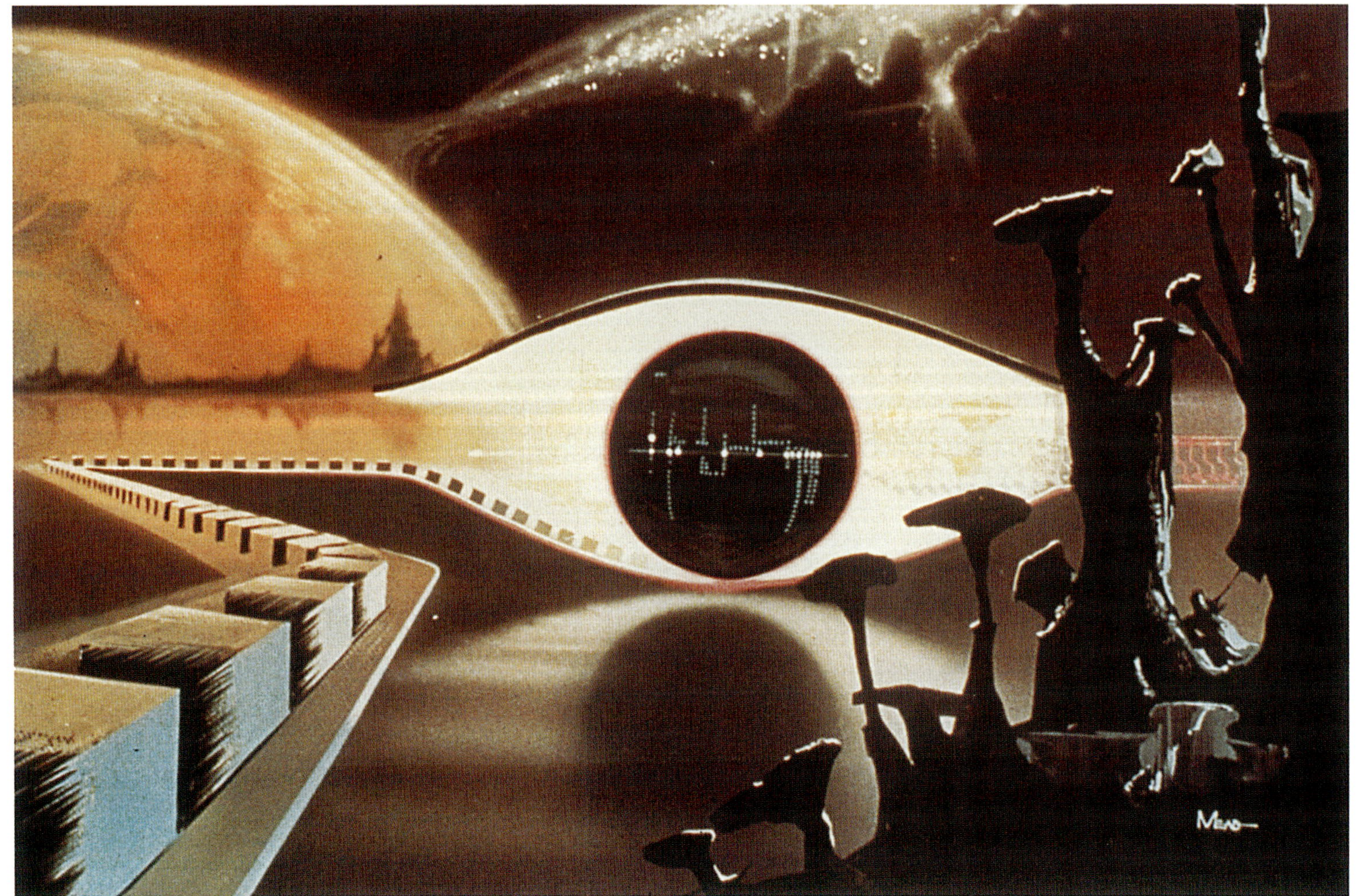

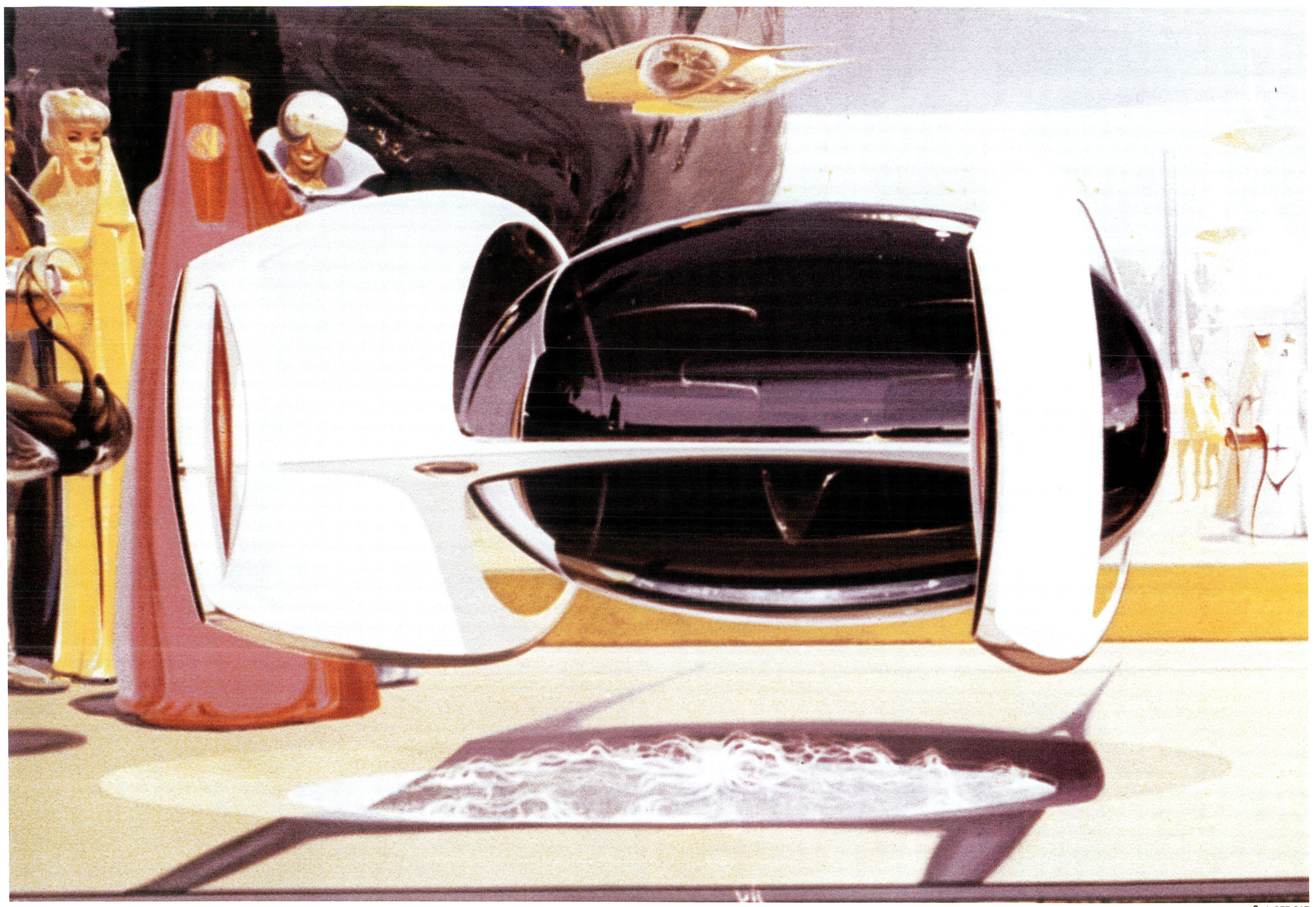

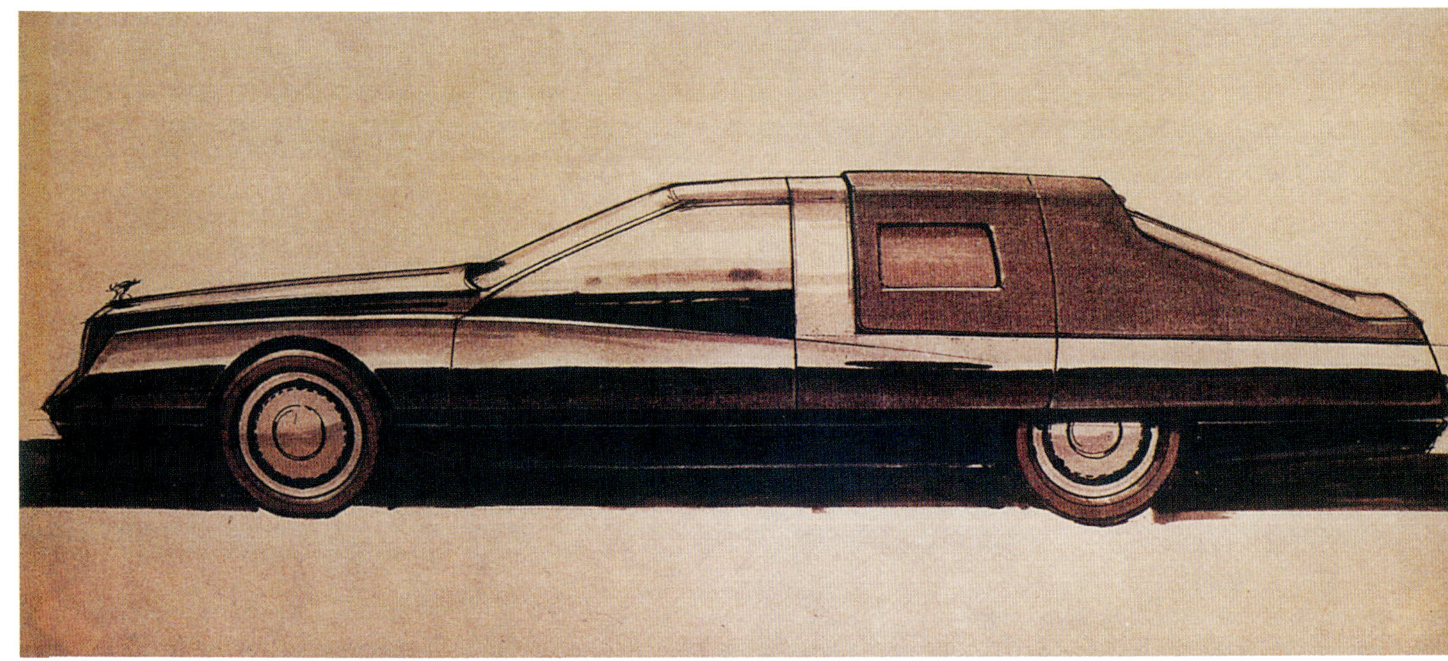

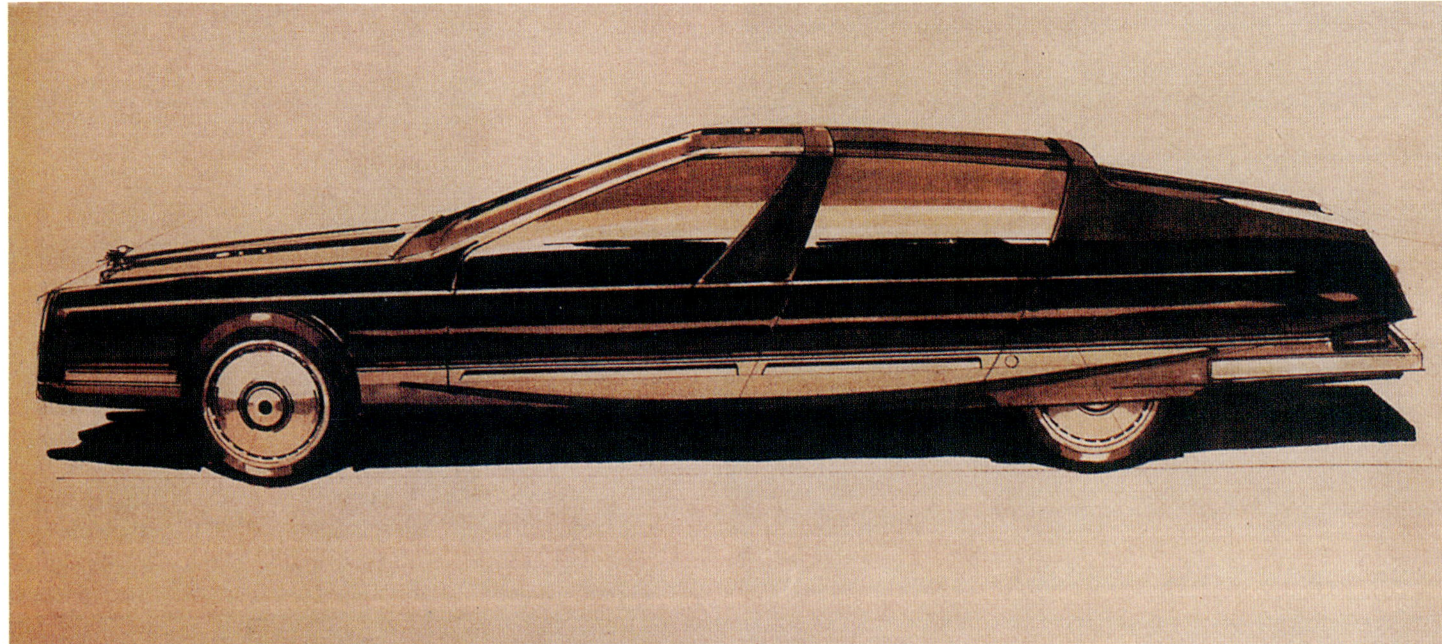

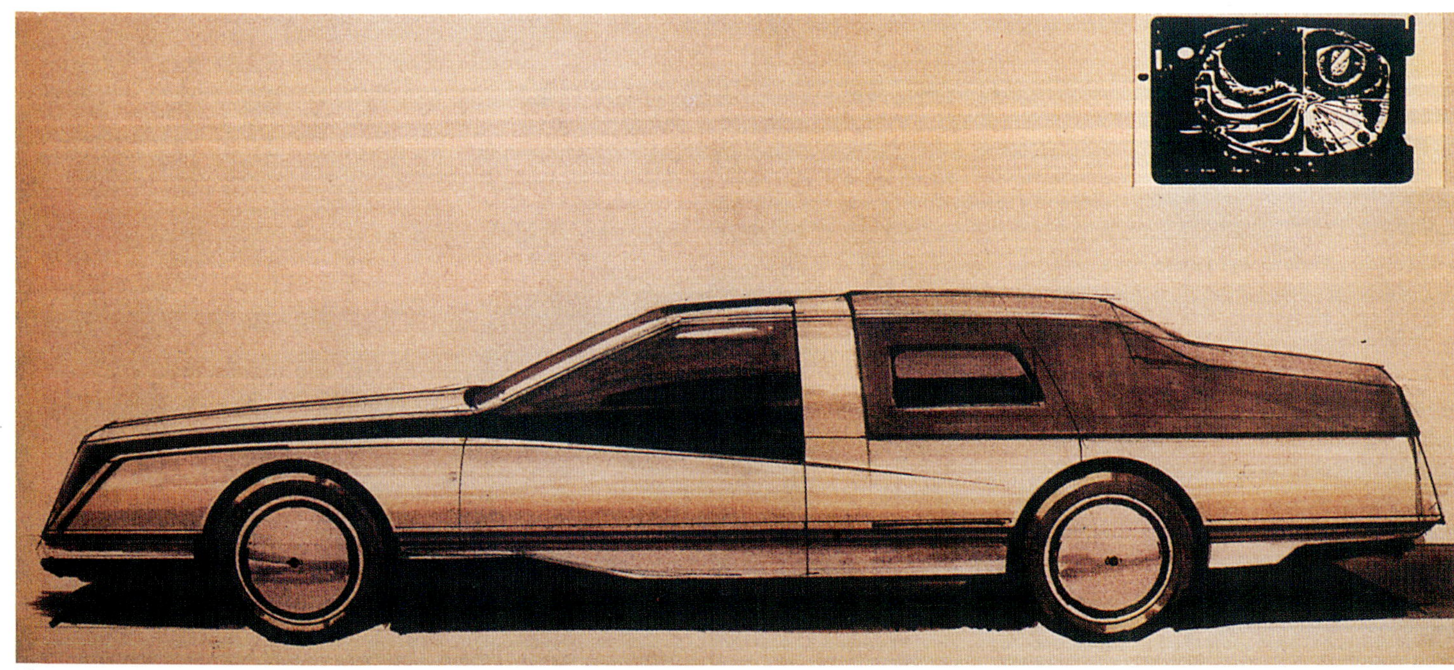

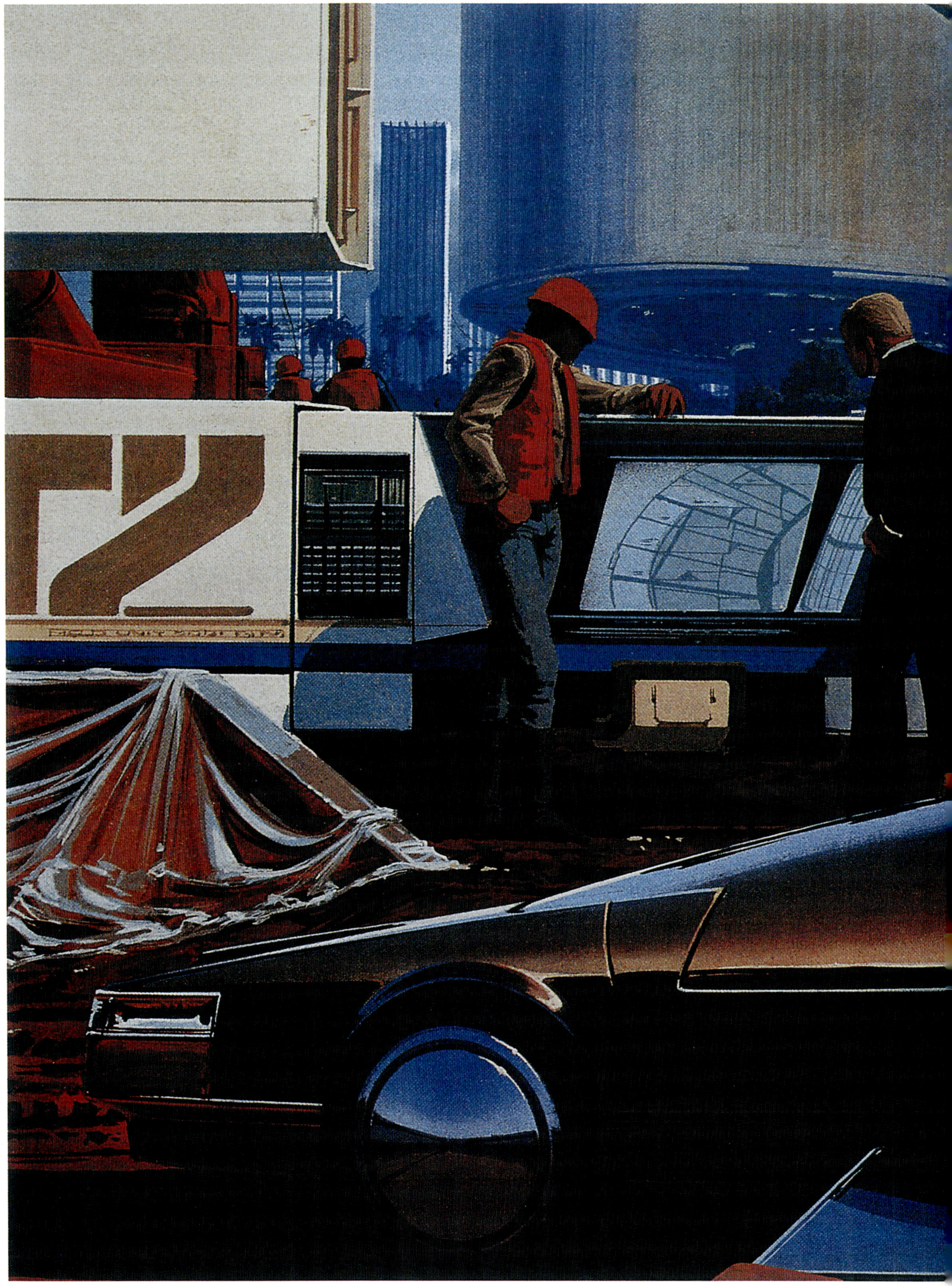

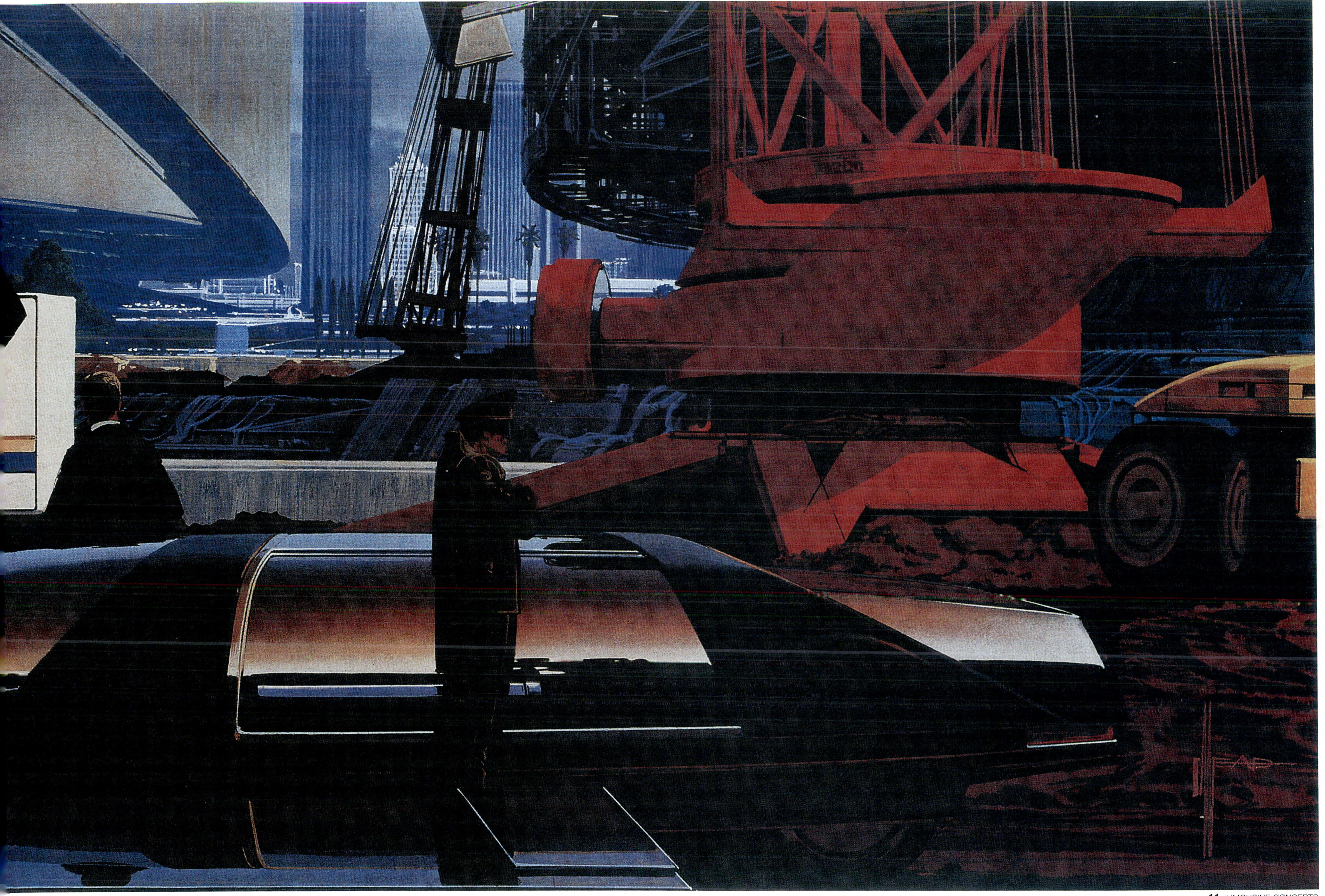

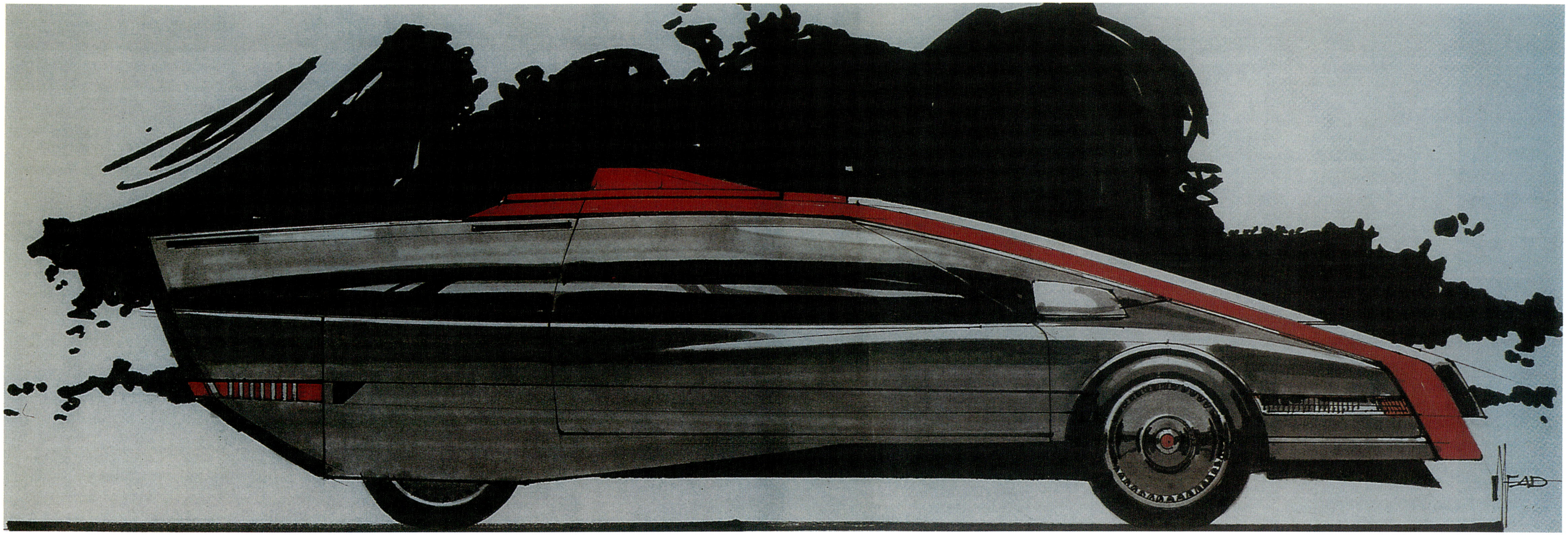

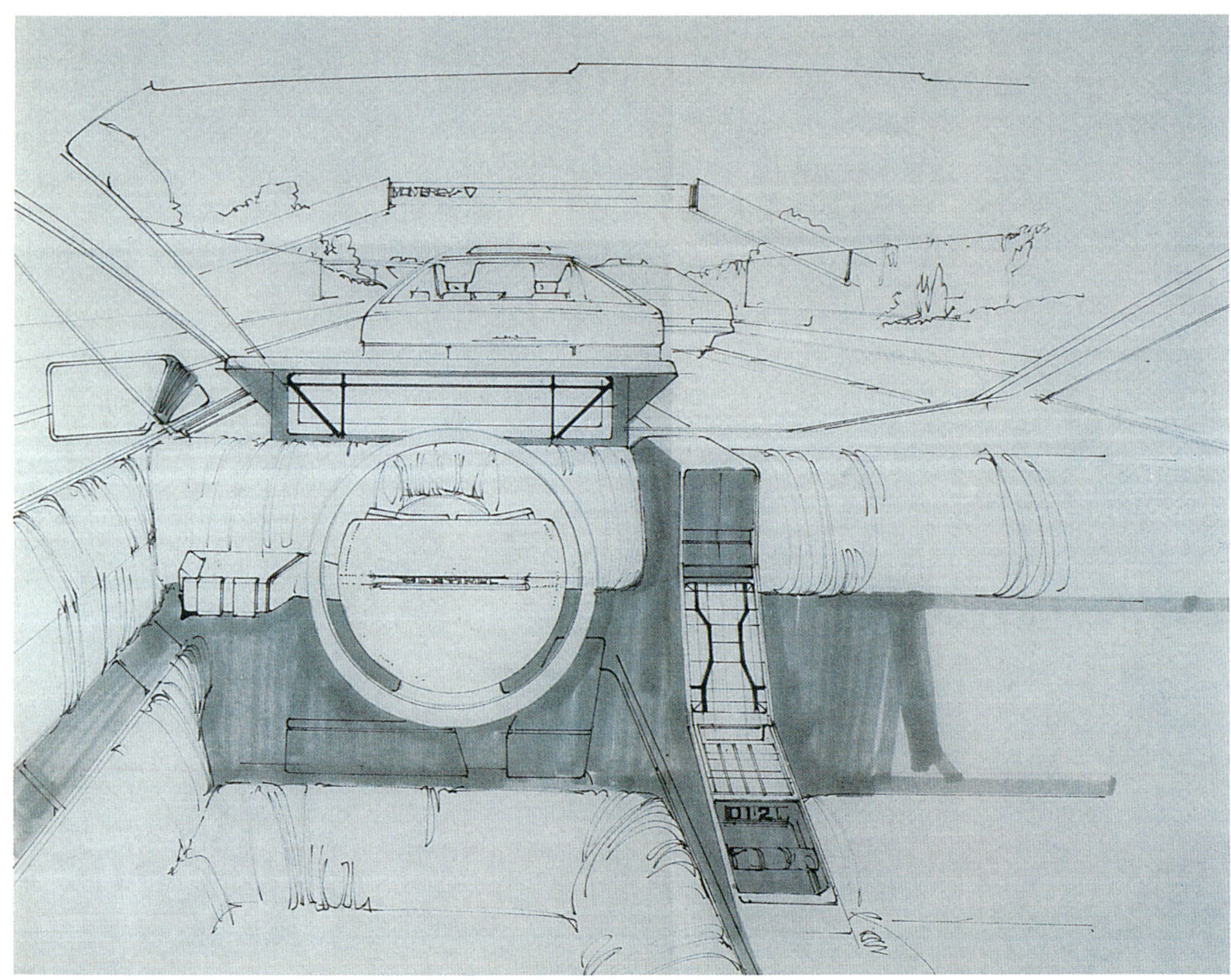

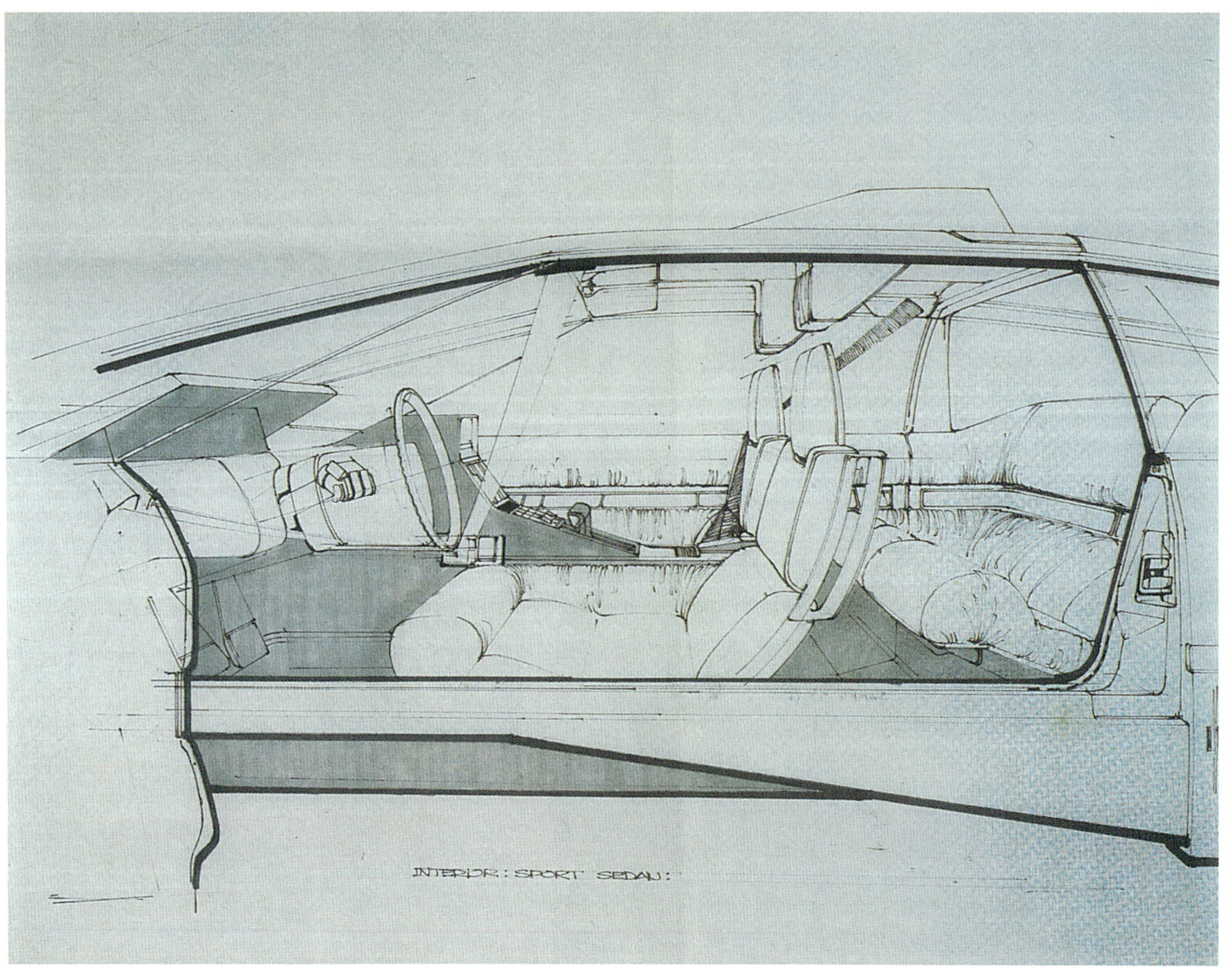

INTERIOR: SPORT SEDAN:

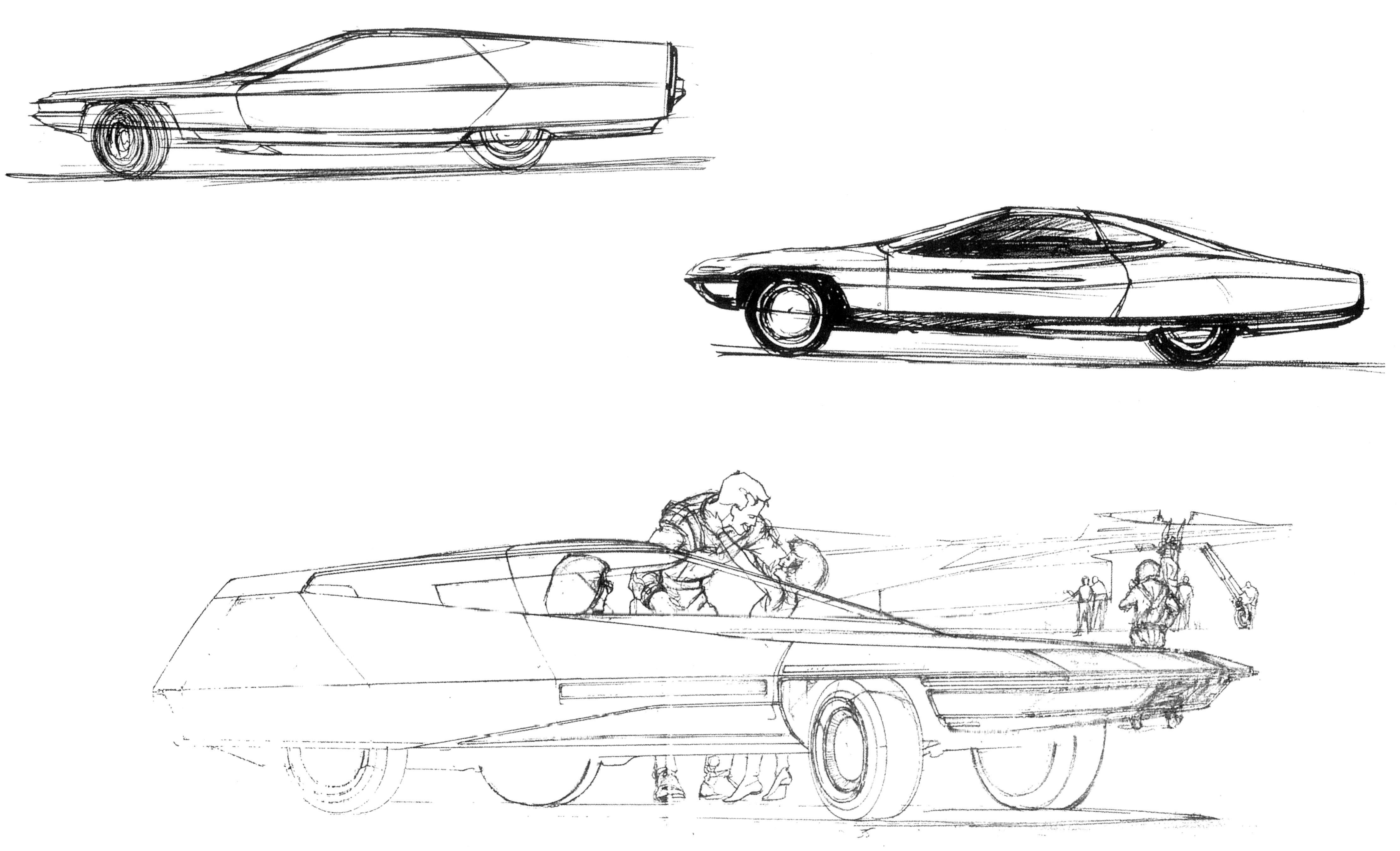

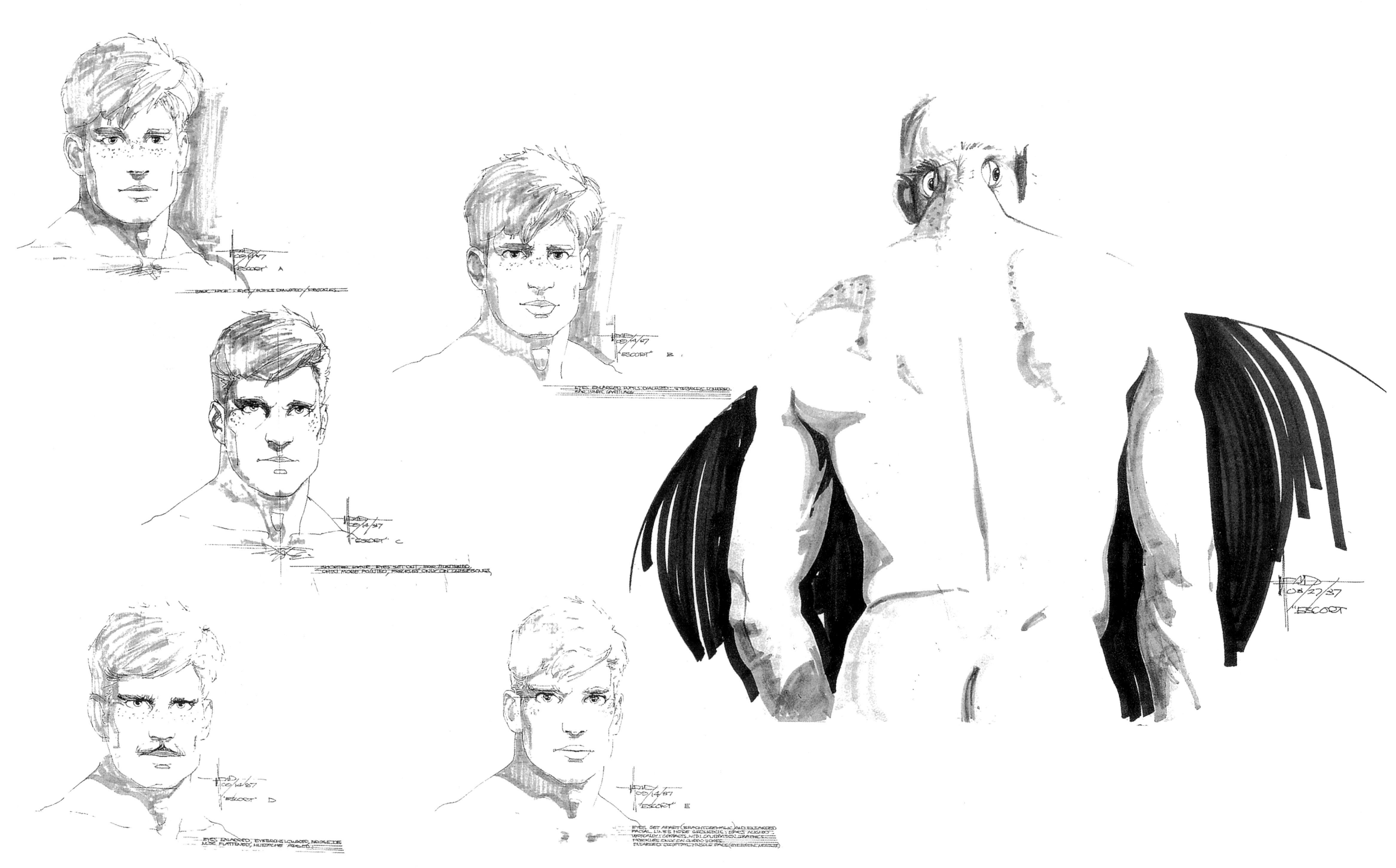

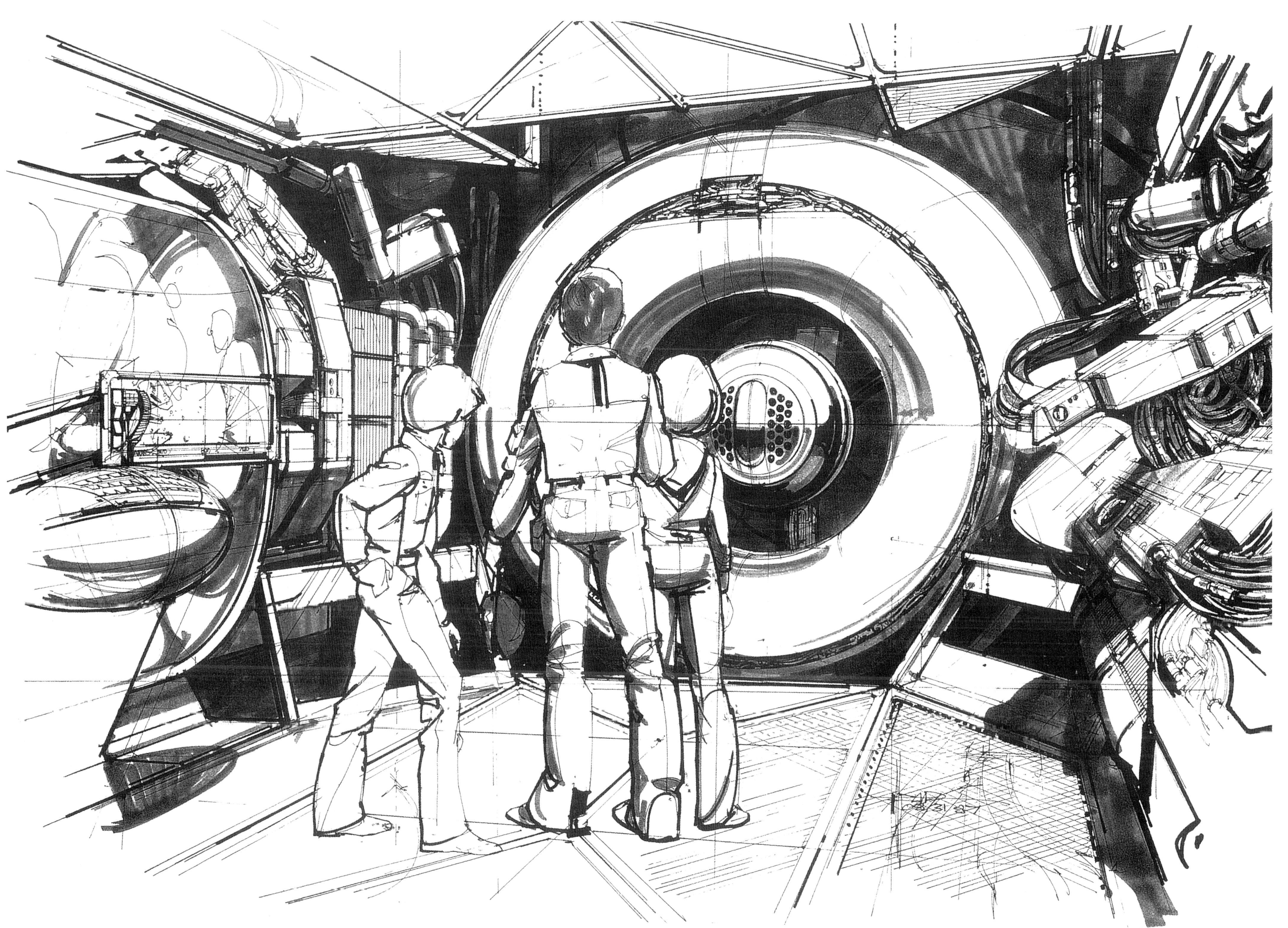

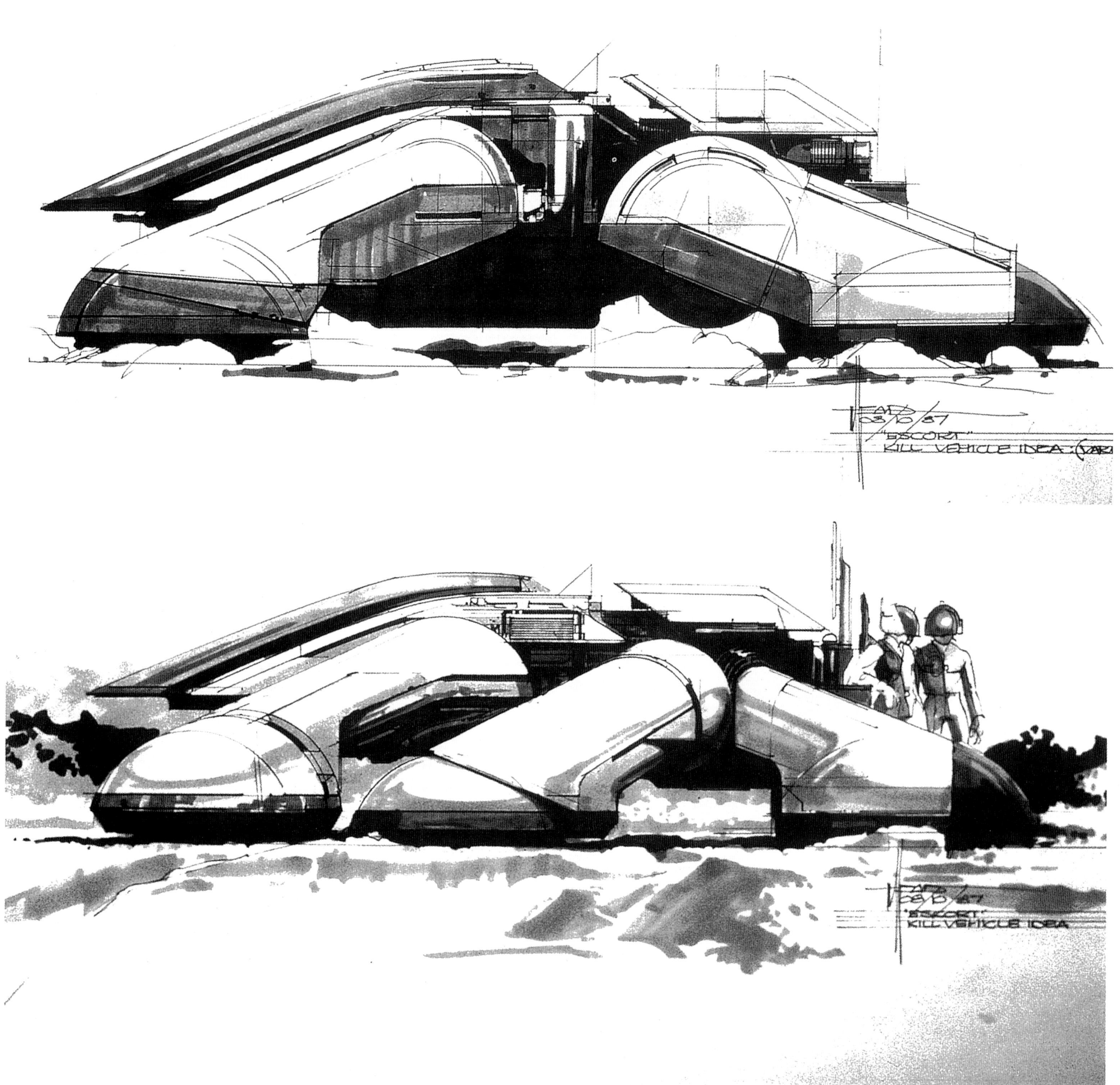
"ESCORT"
KILL VEHICLE IDEA
"ESCORT"
KILL VEHICLE IDEA

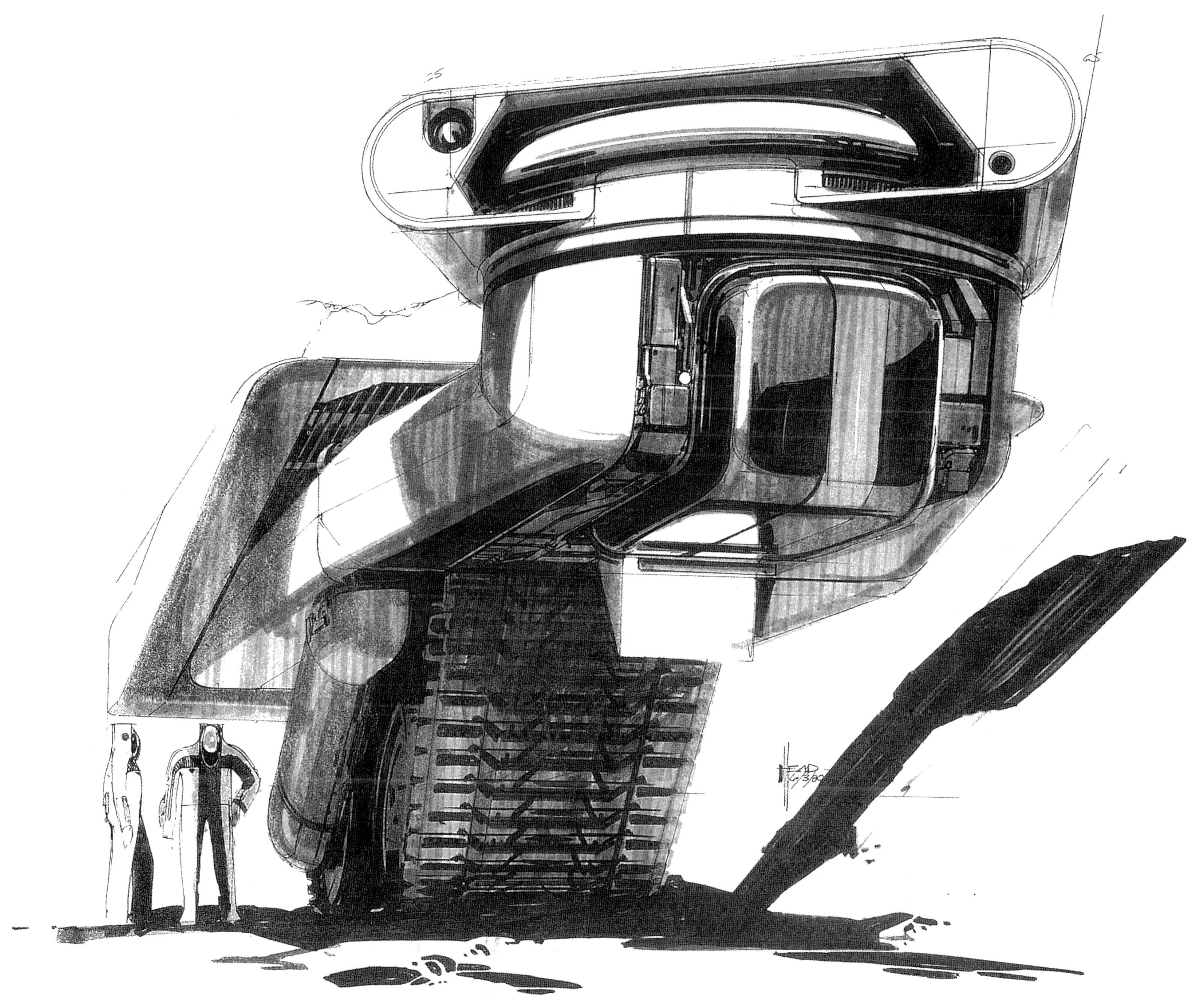

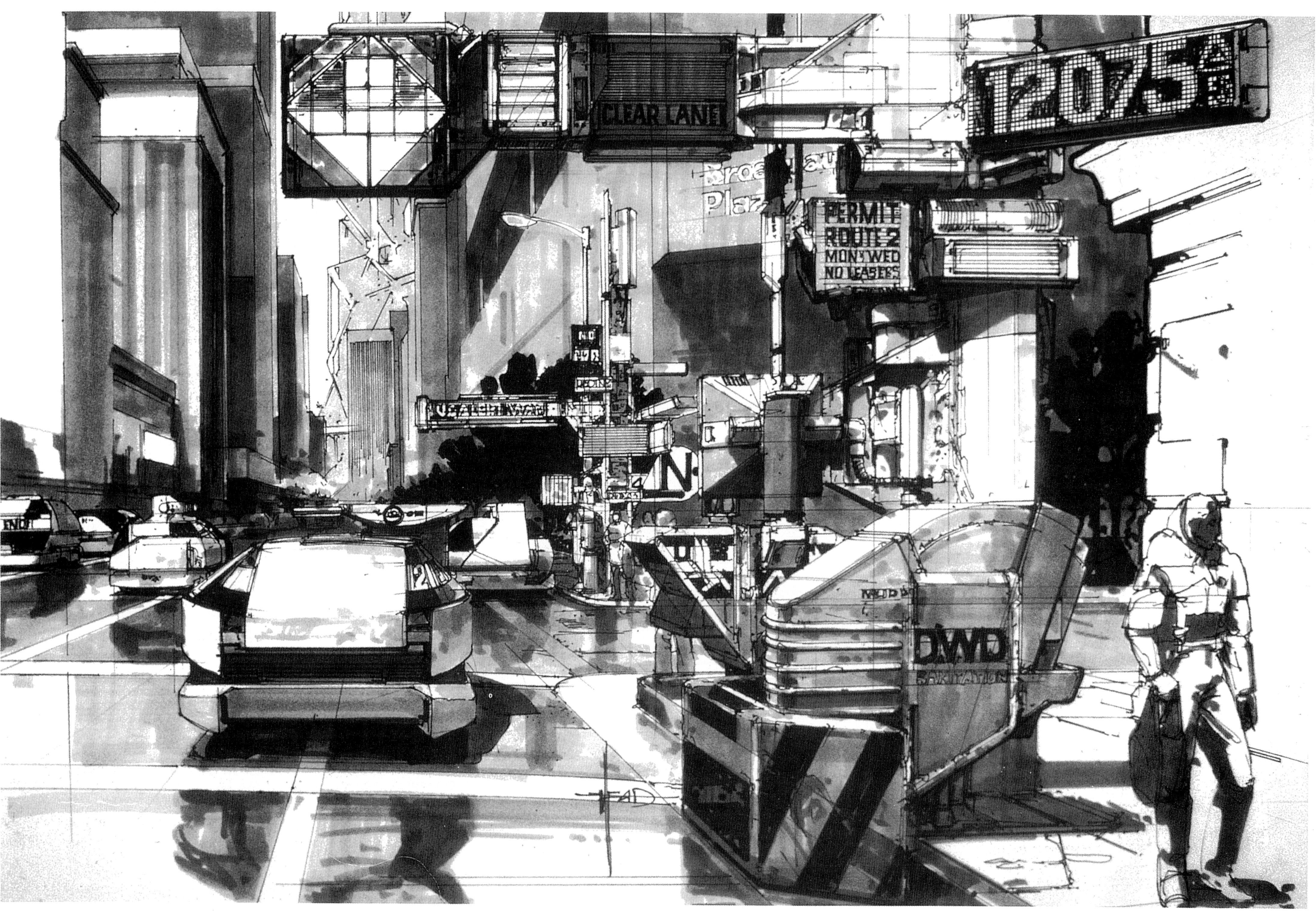

CLEAR LANE
120 75
PERMIT
ROUTE 2
MON & WED
NO LEASES
DWD

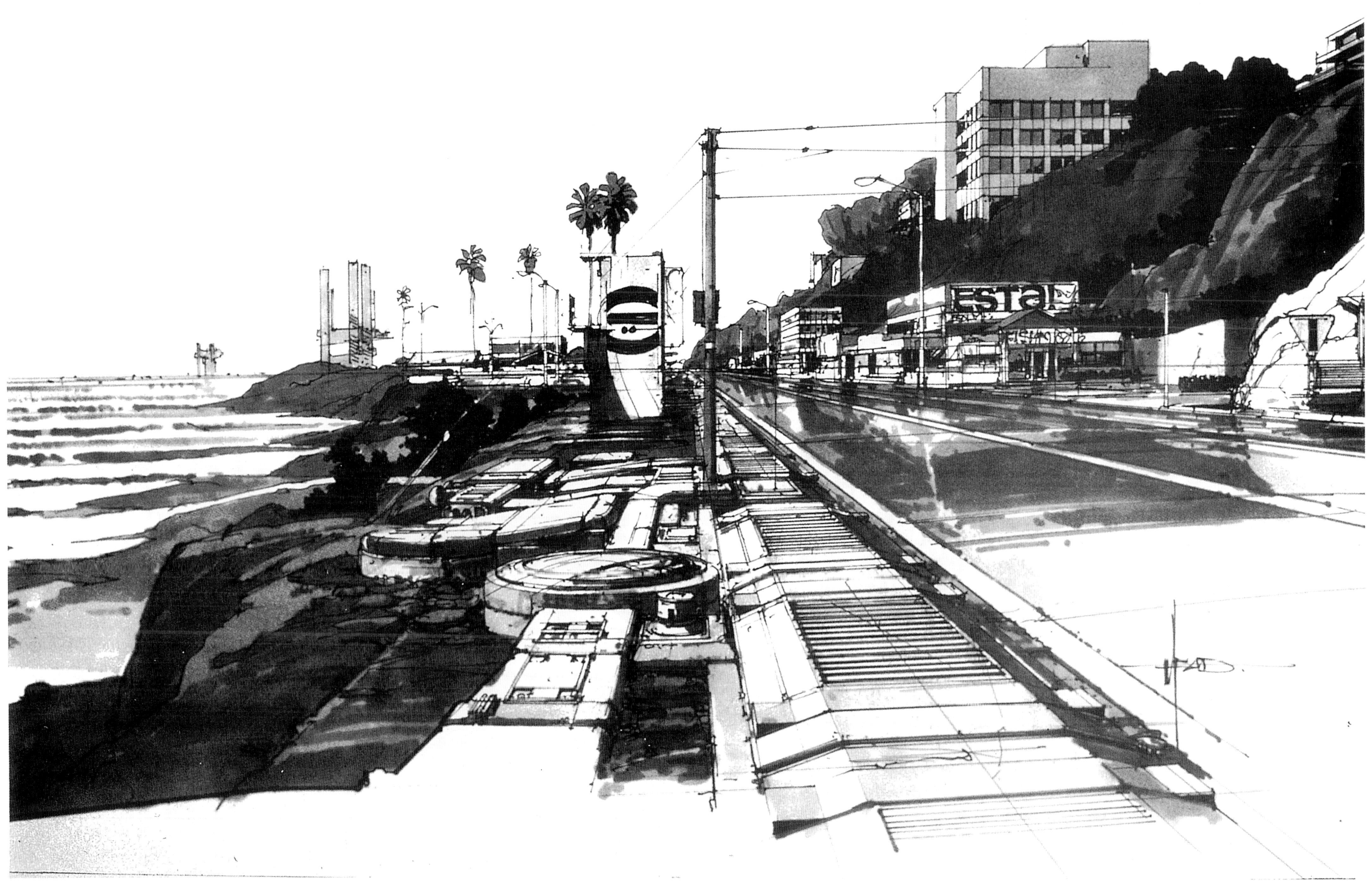

ESTA

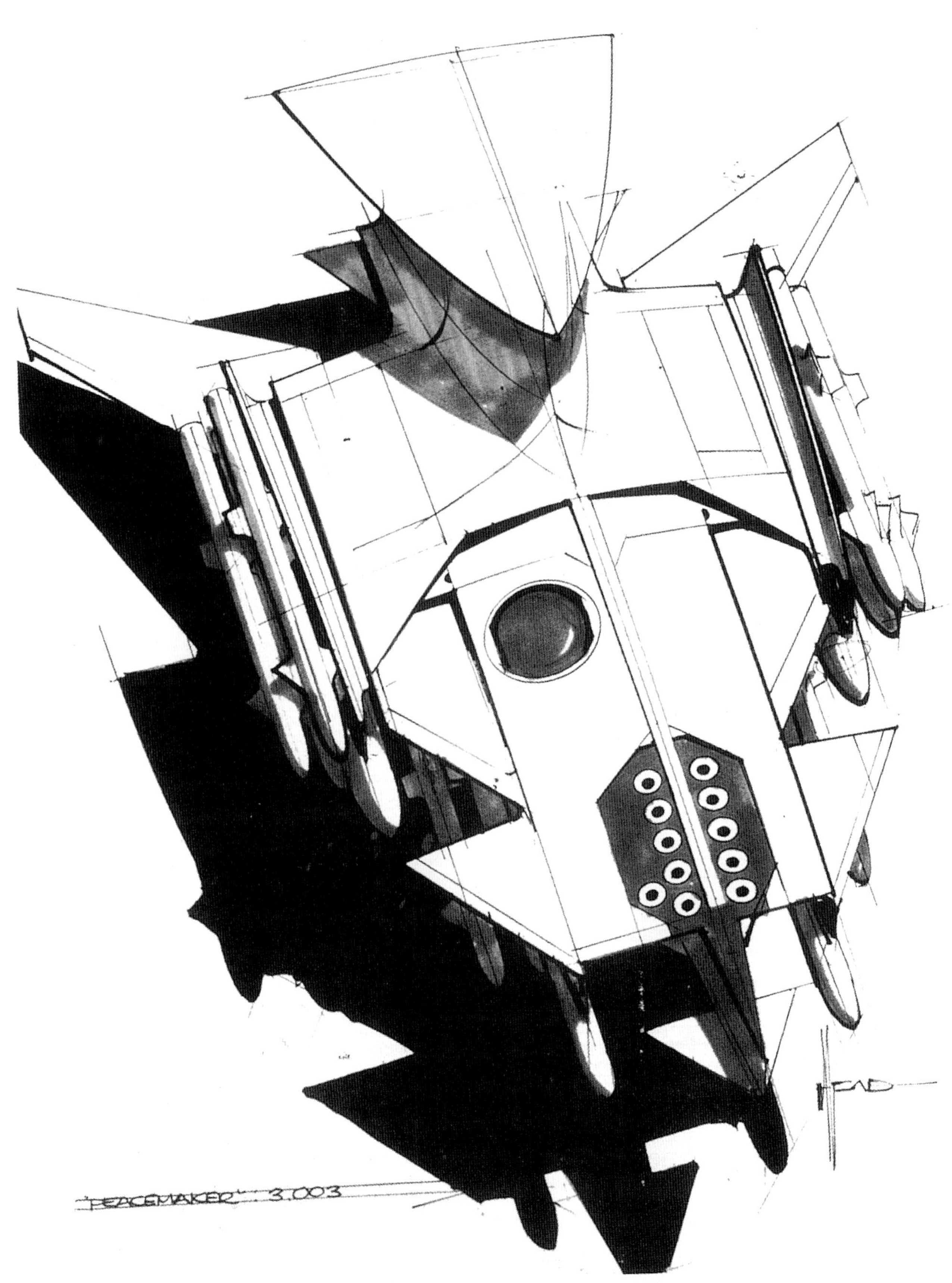

"PEACEMAKER" 3.003

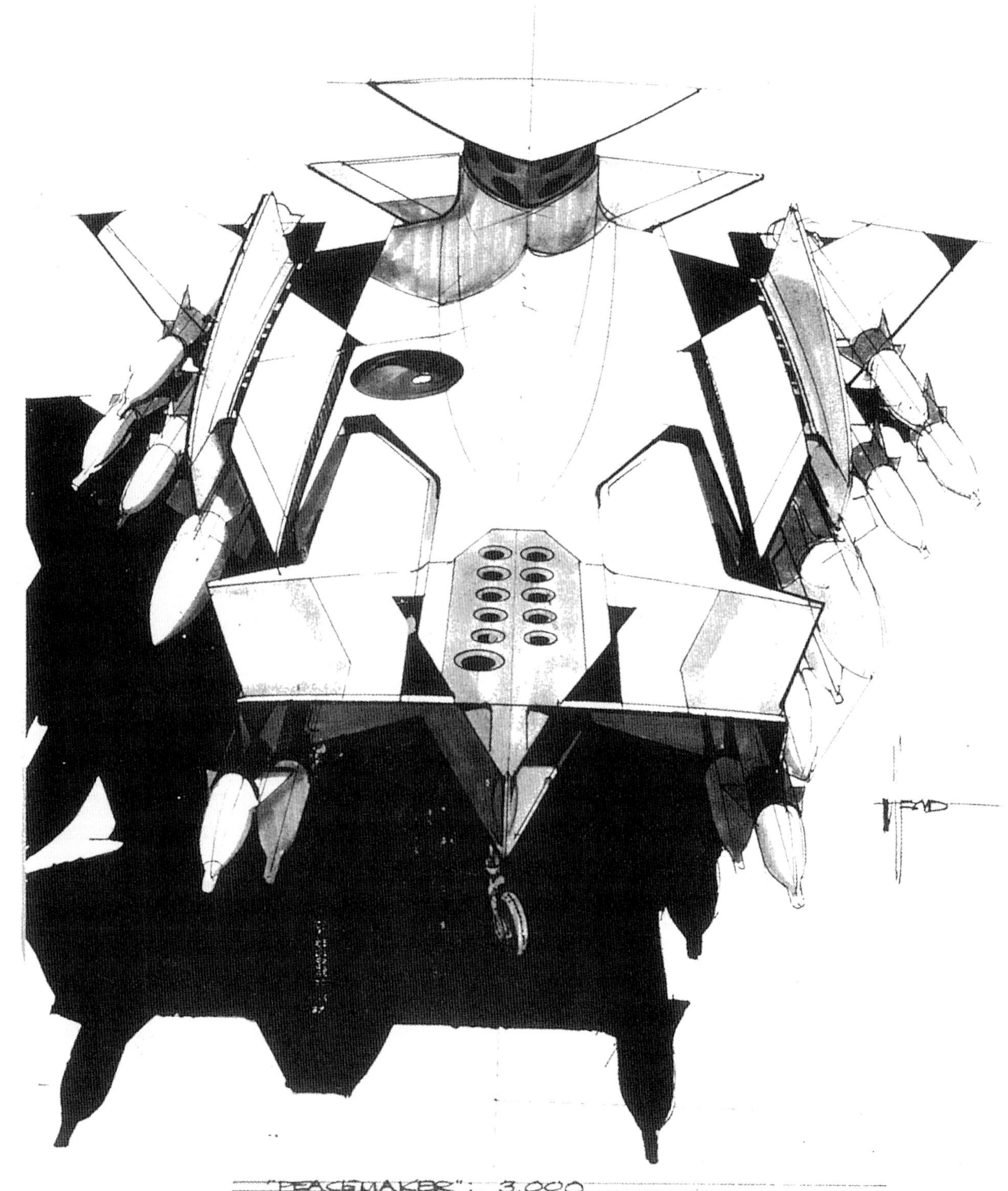

"PEACEMAKER": 3.000

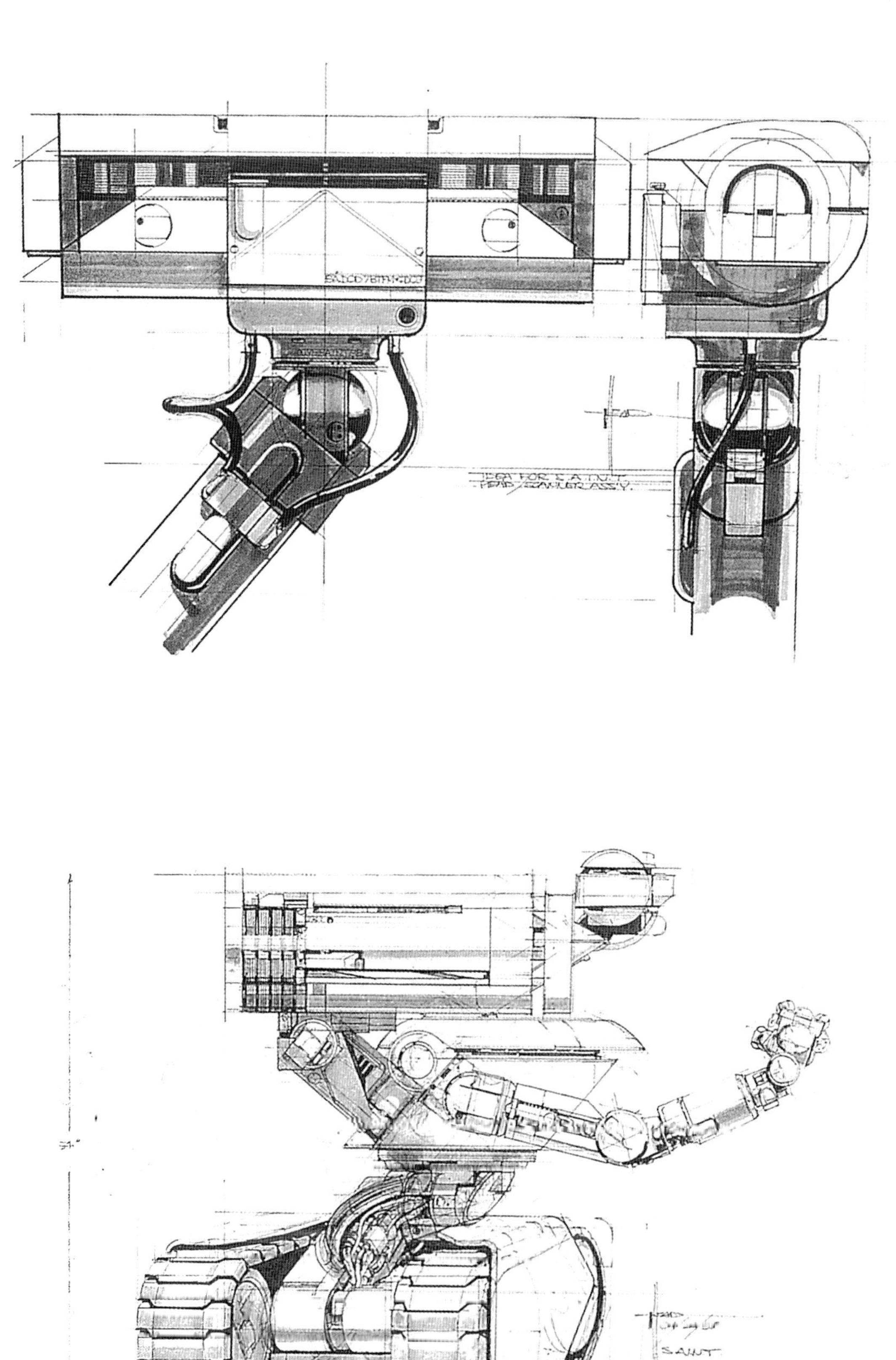
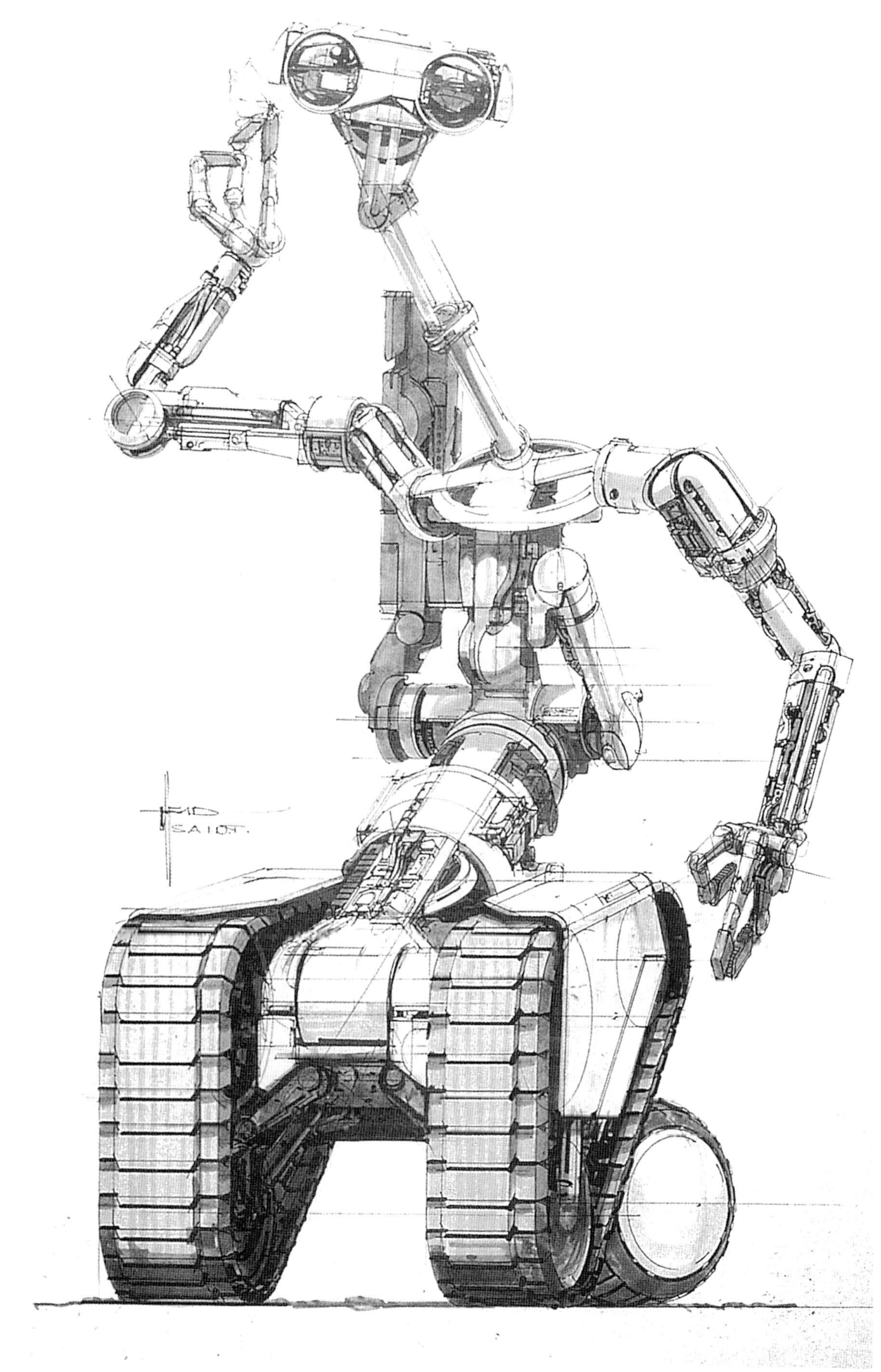

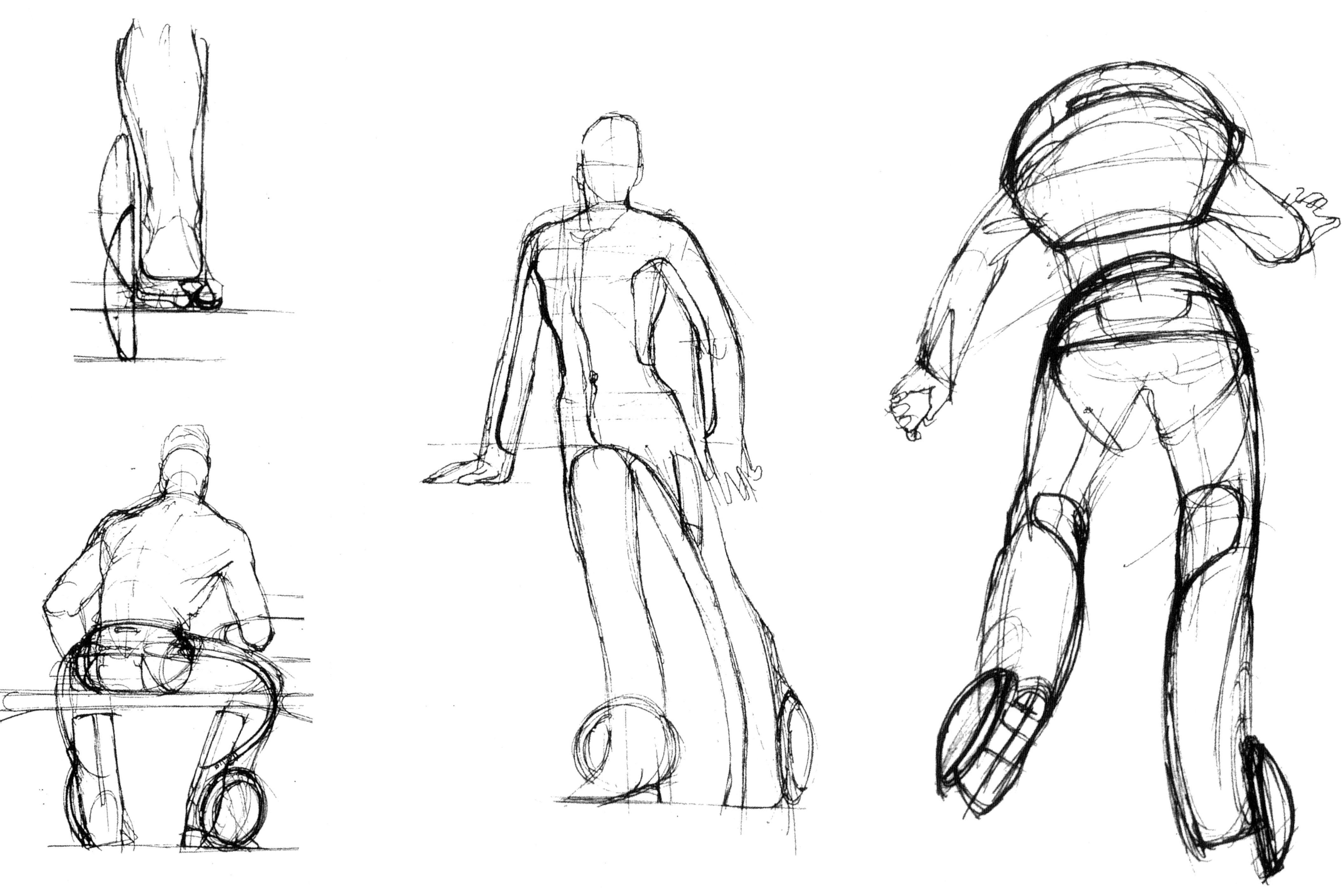

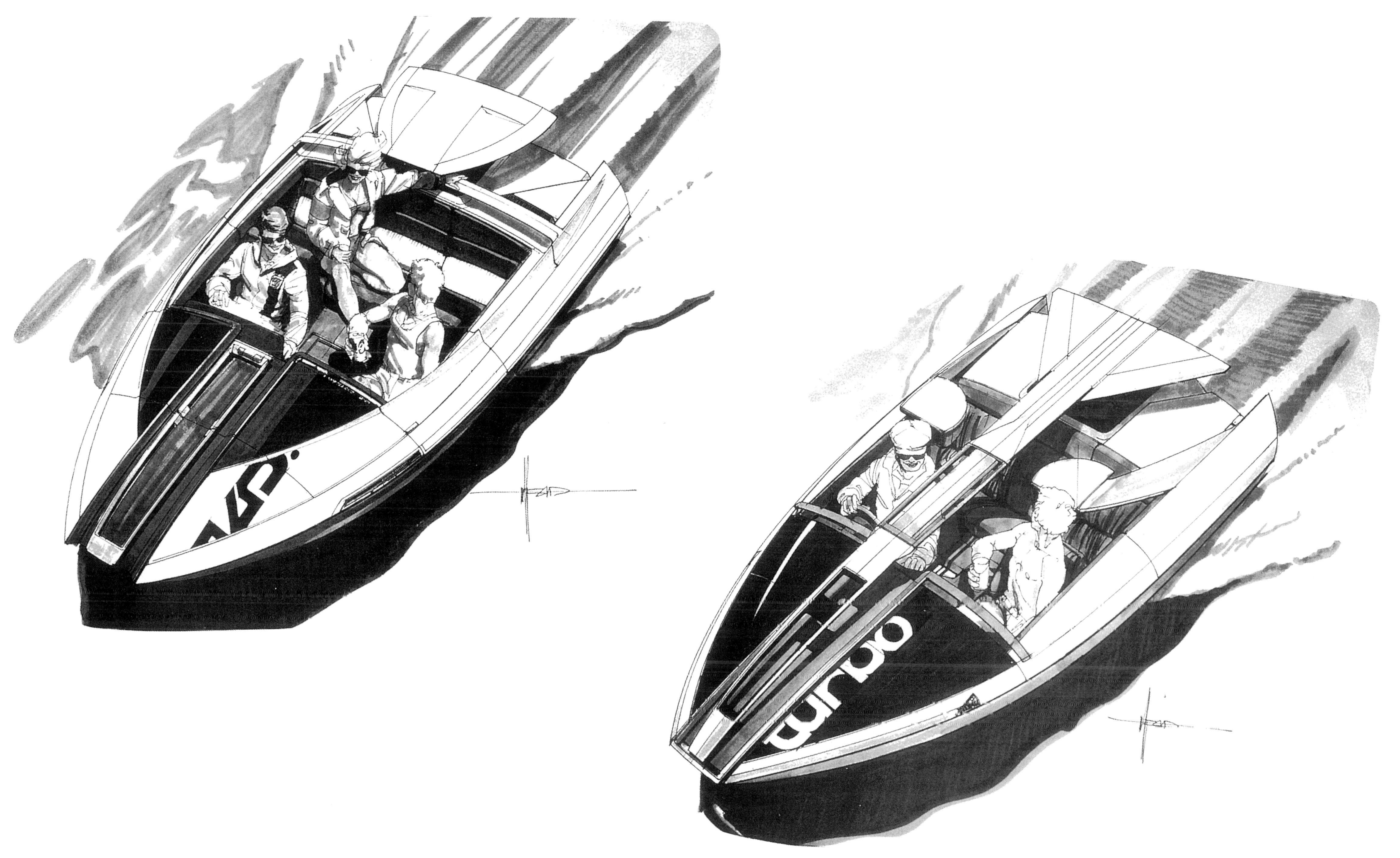

turbo

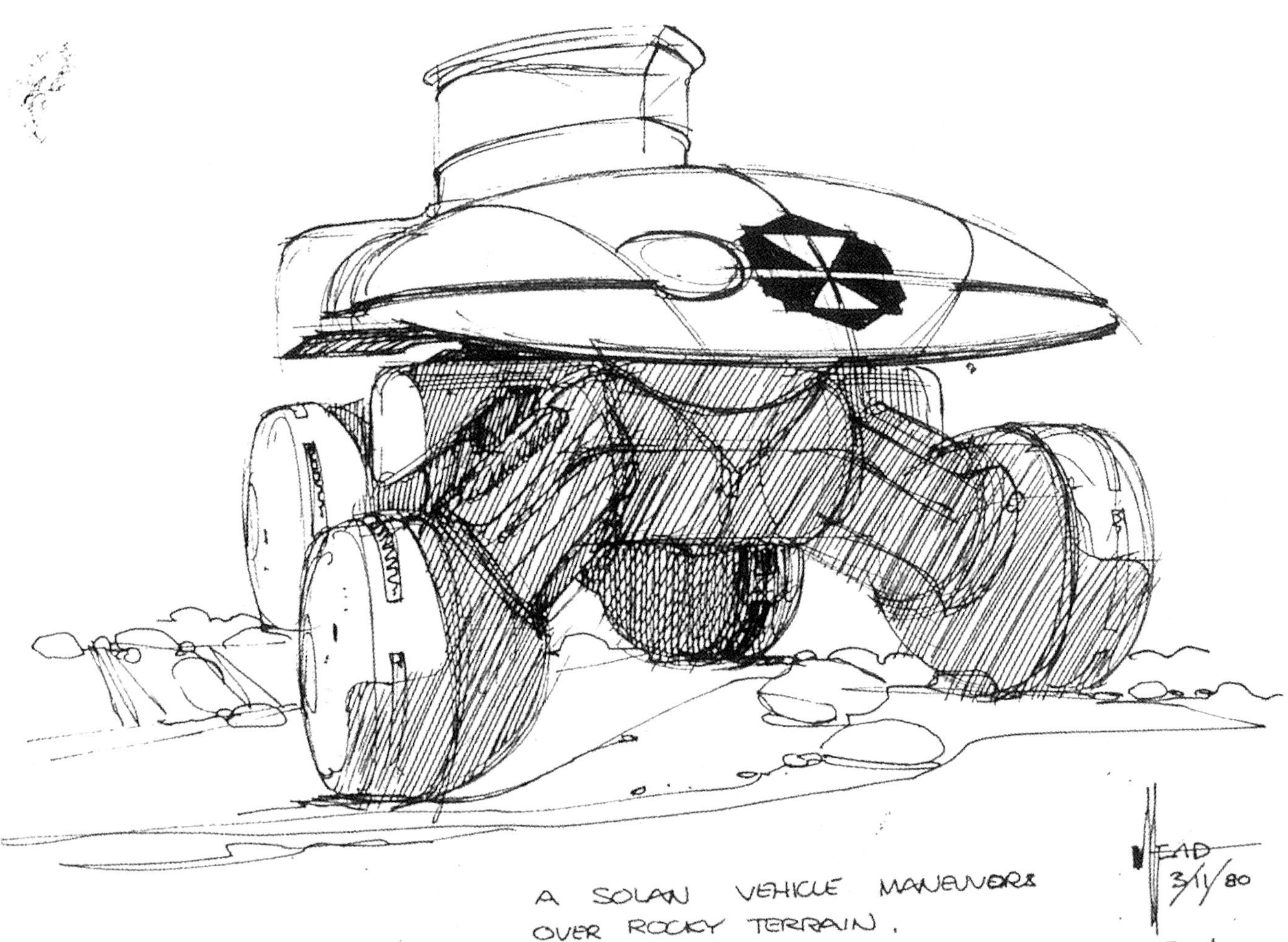

A SOLAR VEHICLE MANEUVERS OVER ROCKY TERRAIN.

(DIFFERENT MORPHOLOGY: SAME GENESIS. IN
BODY PLATES, ARTICULATION, ETC. : AS IN
A CRAB TO A DOLPHIN, ETC. : EVOLUTION RE-ARRANGES
STANDARD "SYSTEM" TO FIT PREDATORY/RUMINANT DIFFERENCE!)

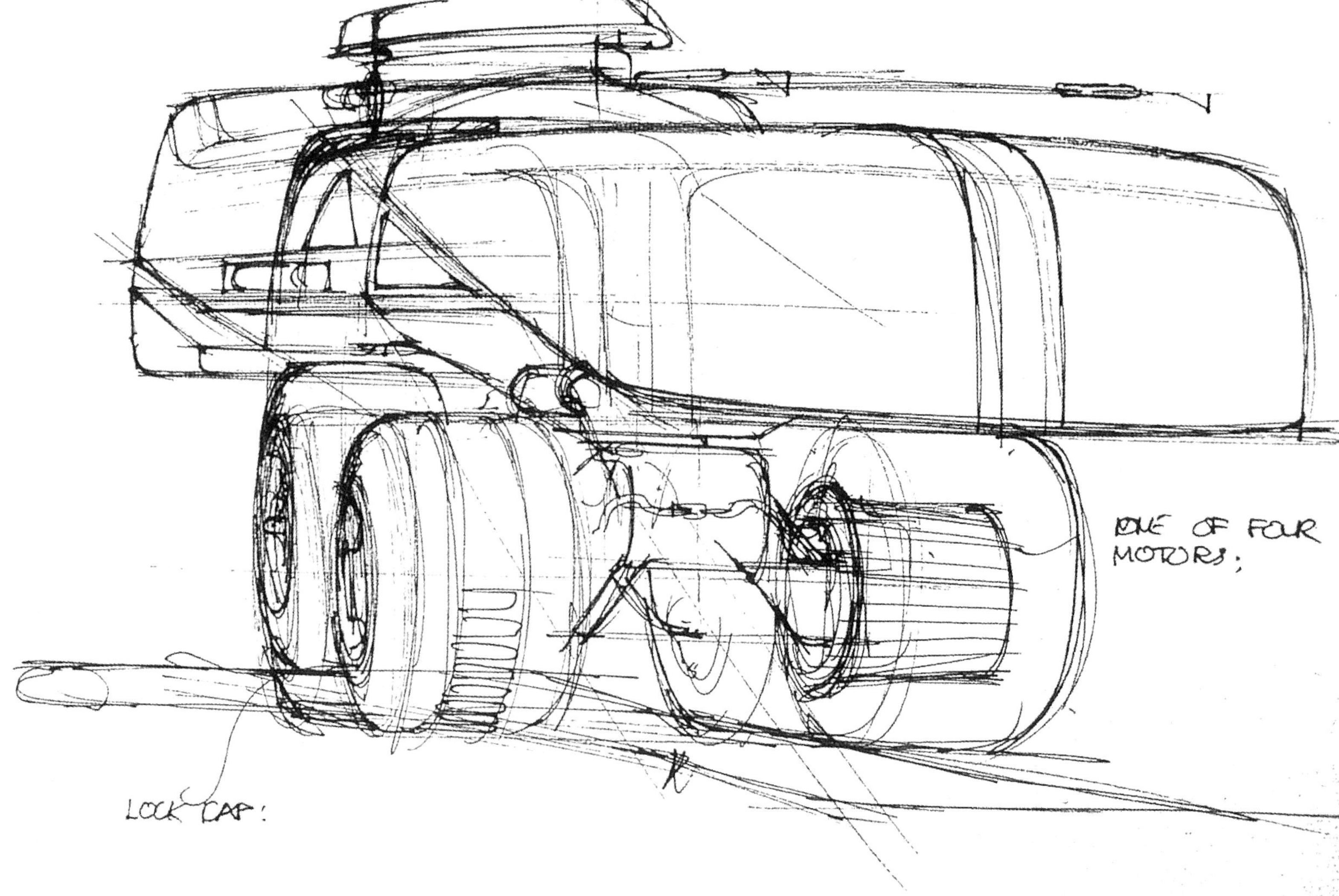

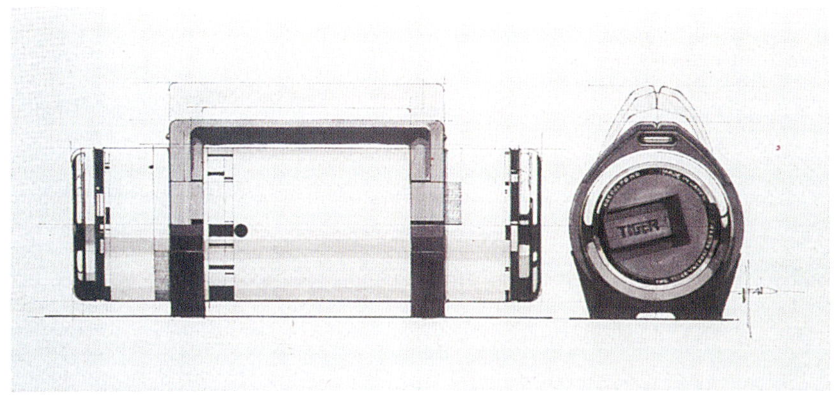
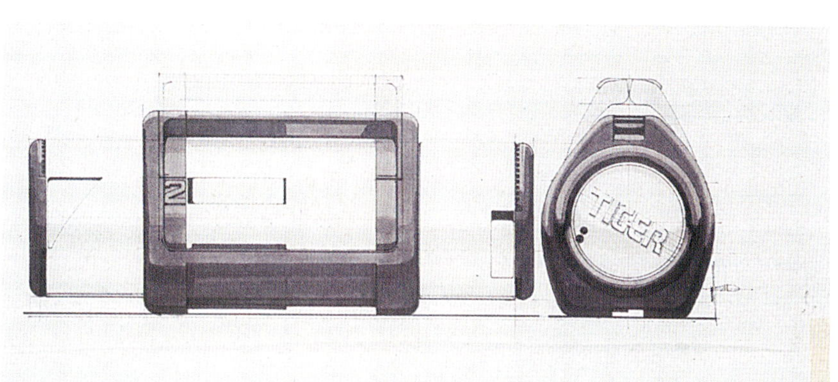
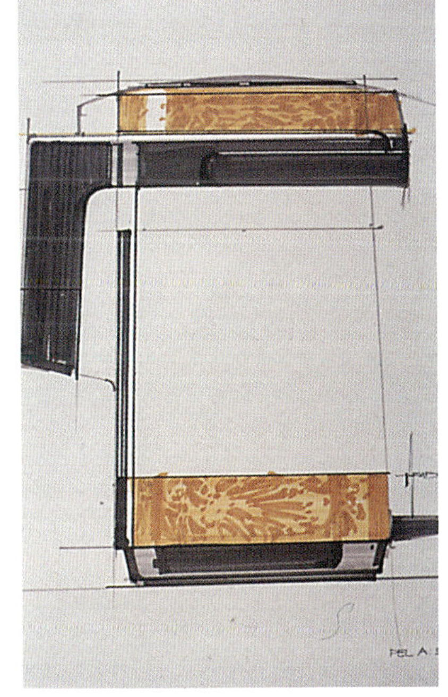
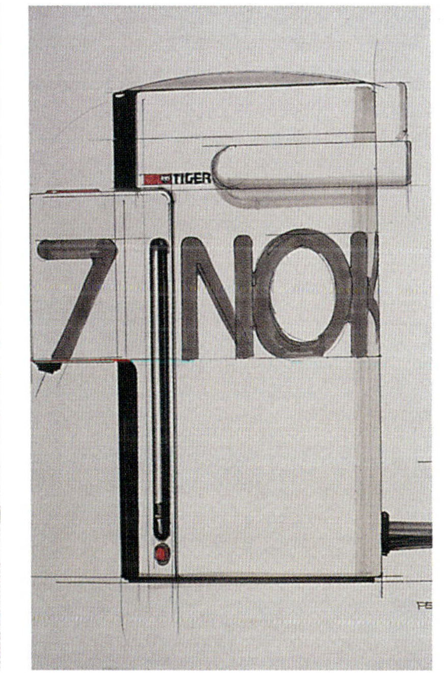
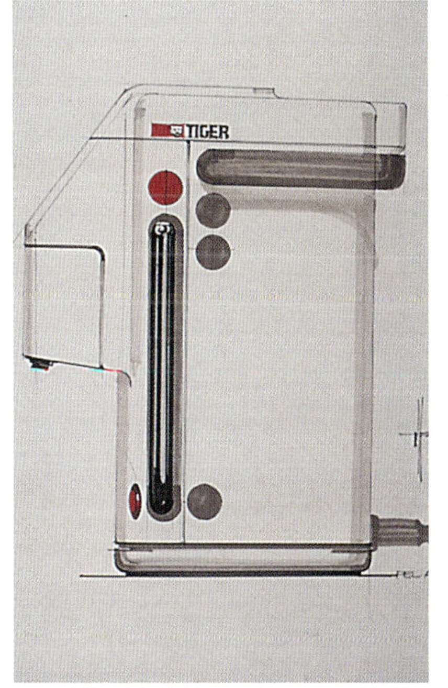
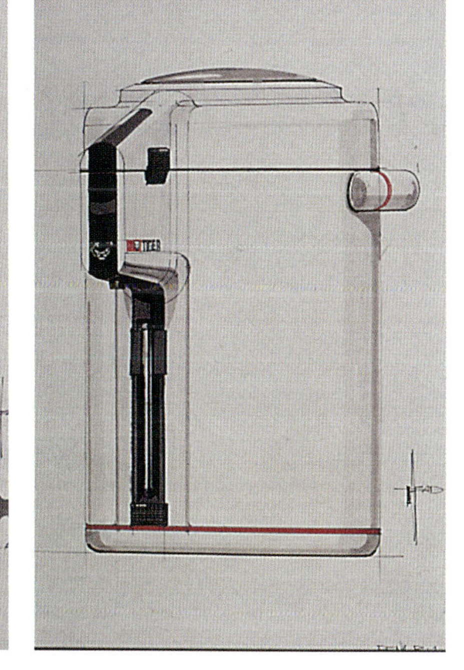
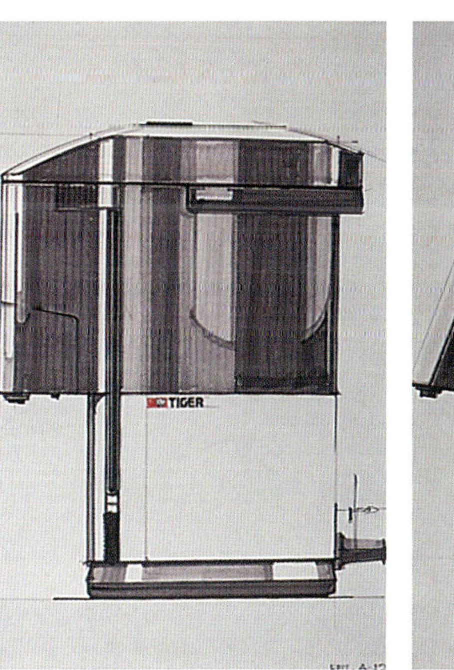
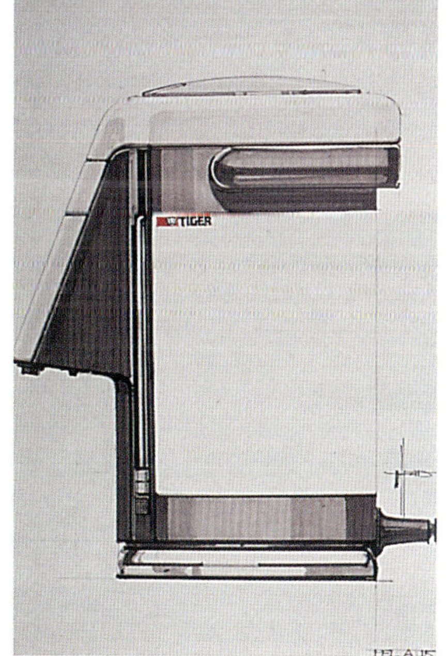
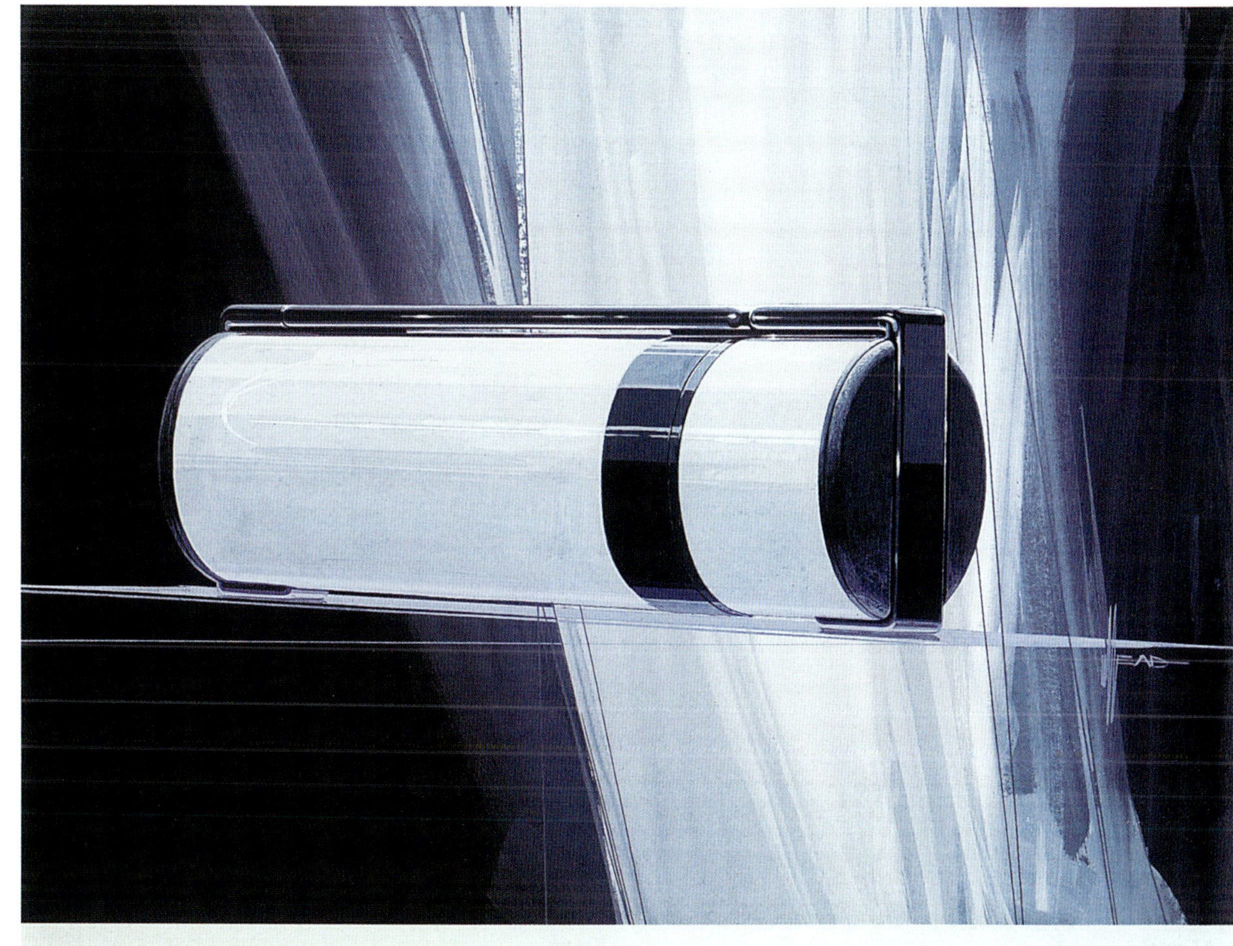
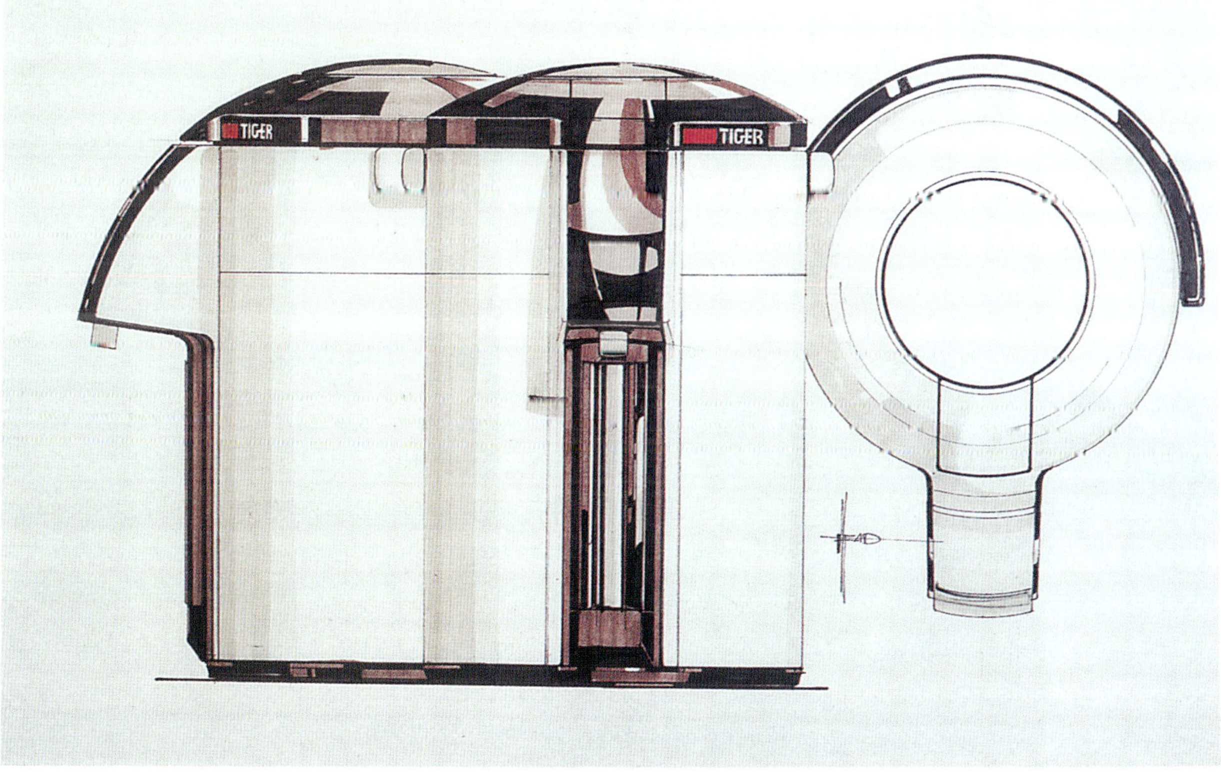

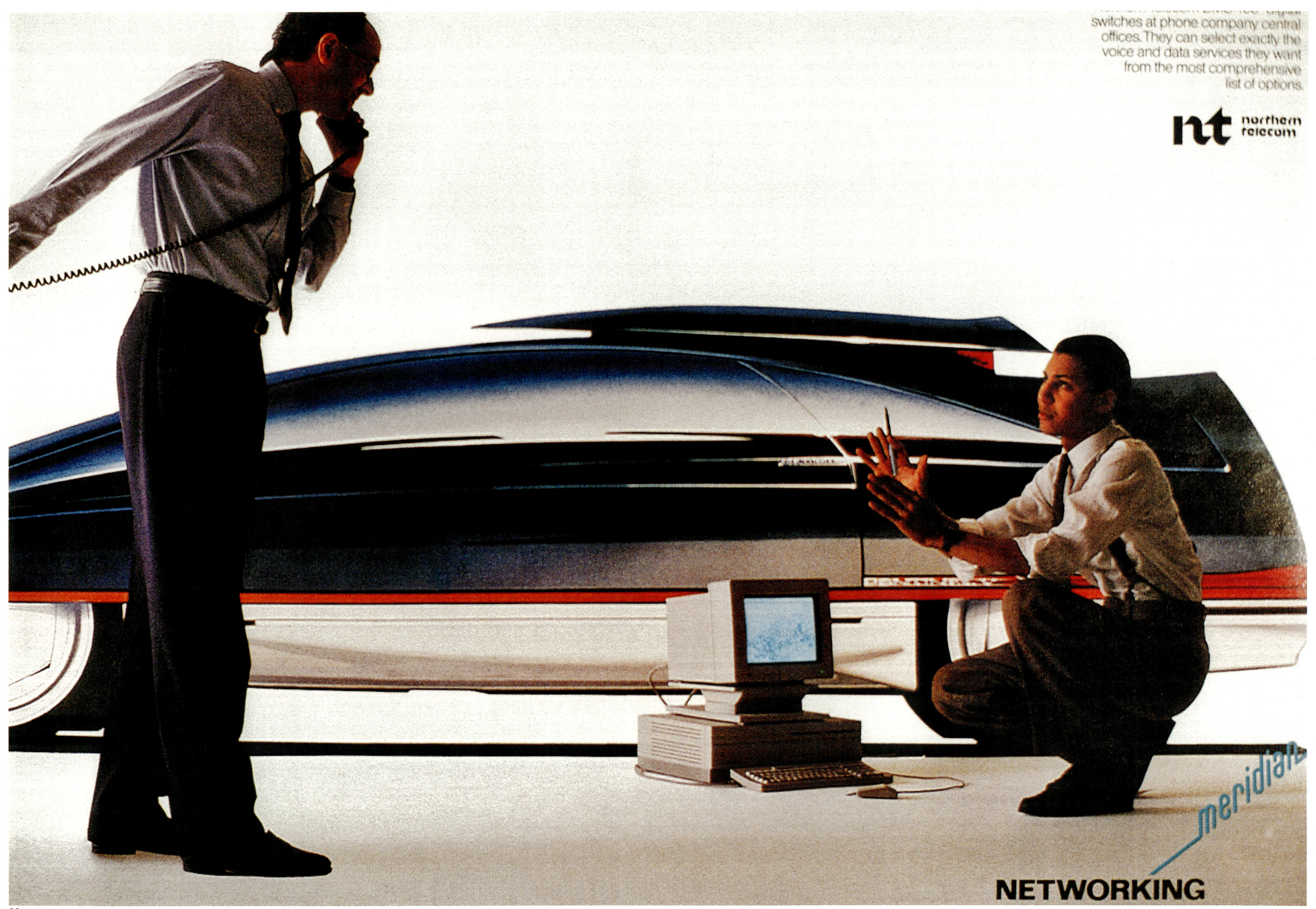
switches at phone company central
offices. They can select exactly the
voice and data services they want
from the most comprehensive
list of options.

nt northern telecom

meridian

NETWORKING

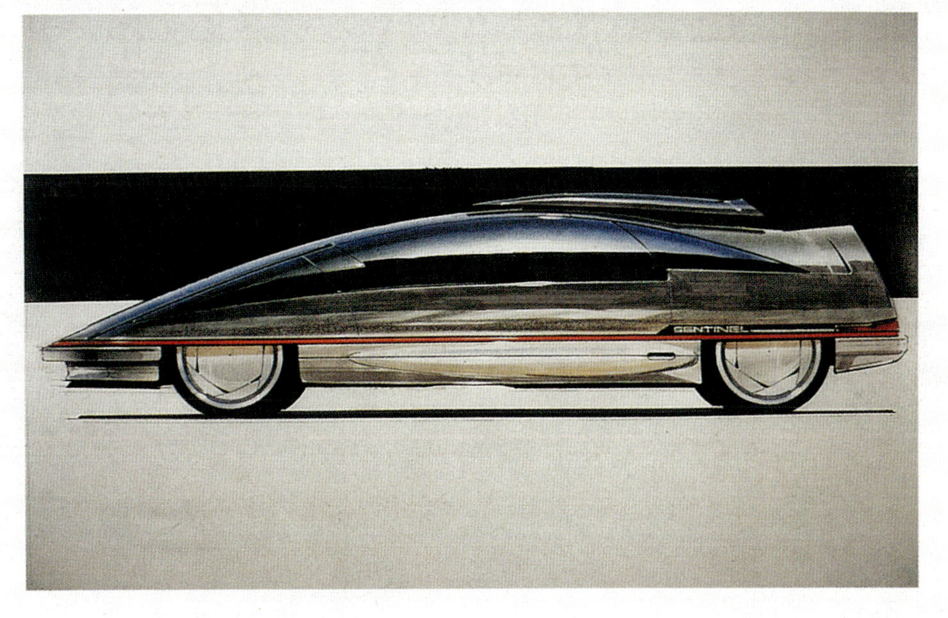

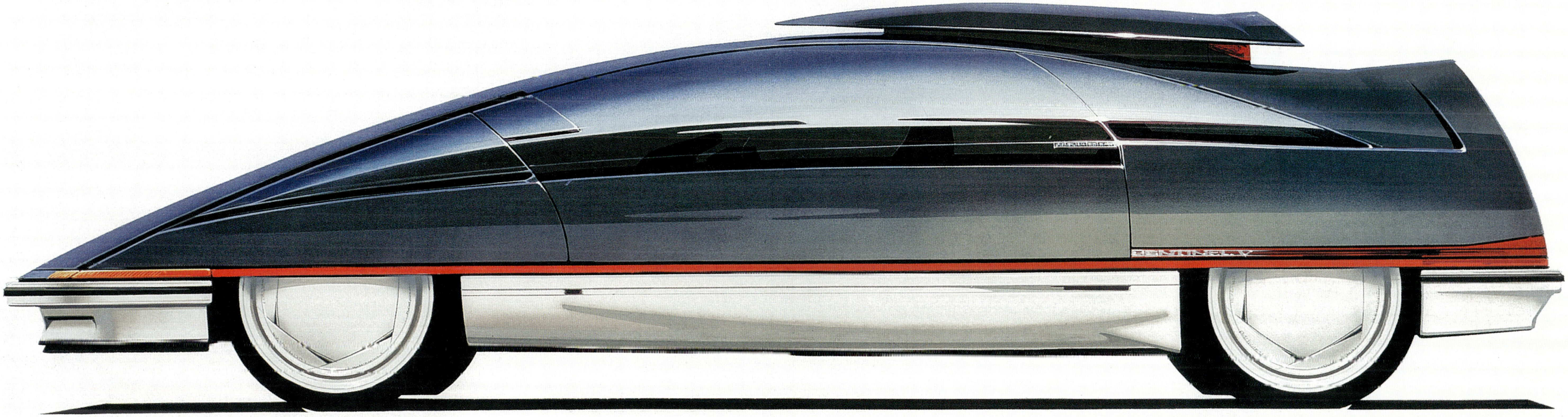

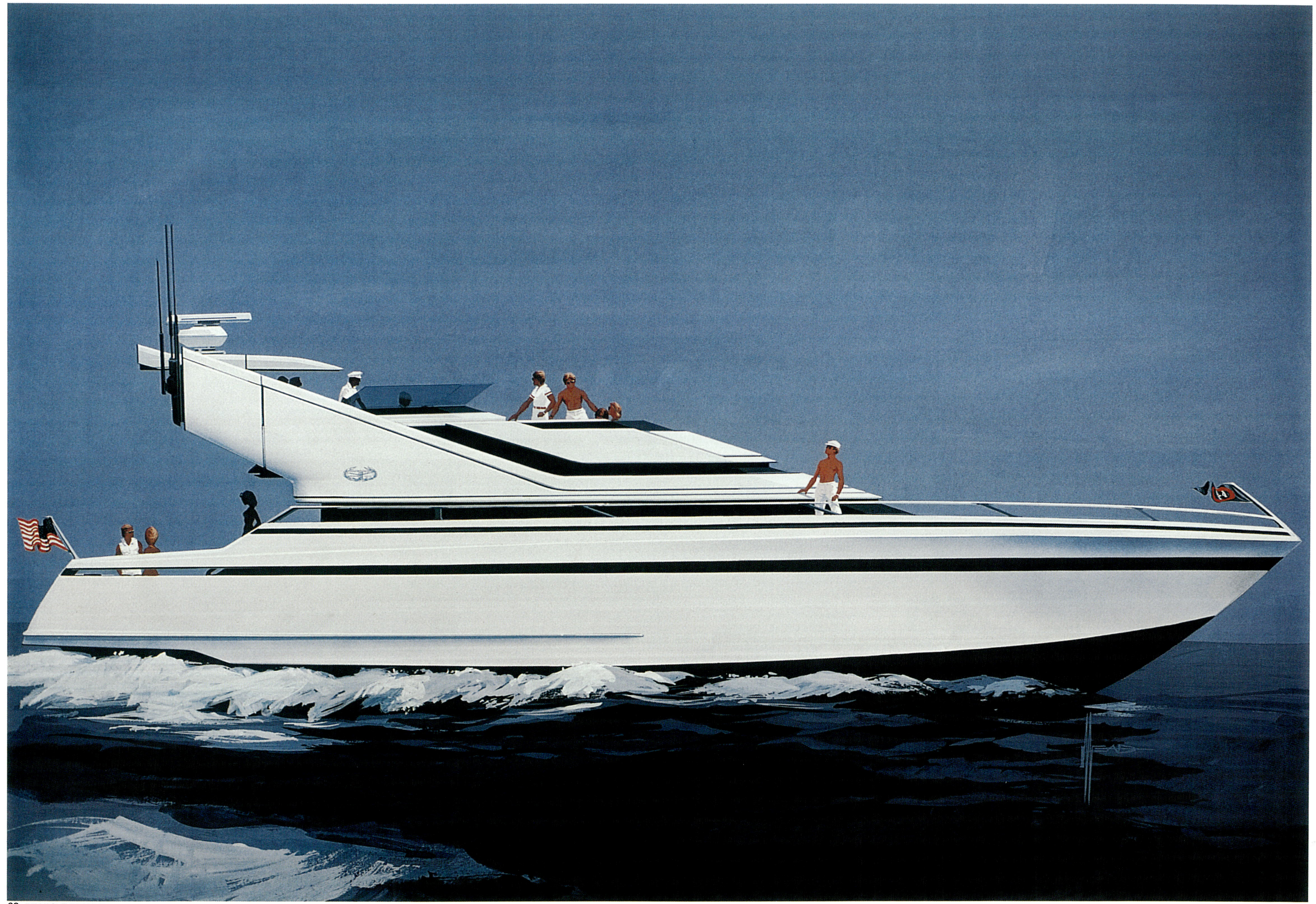

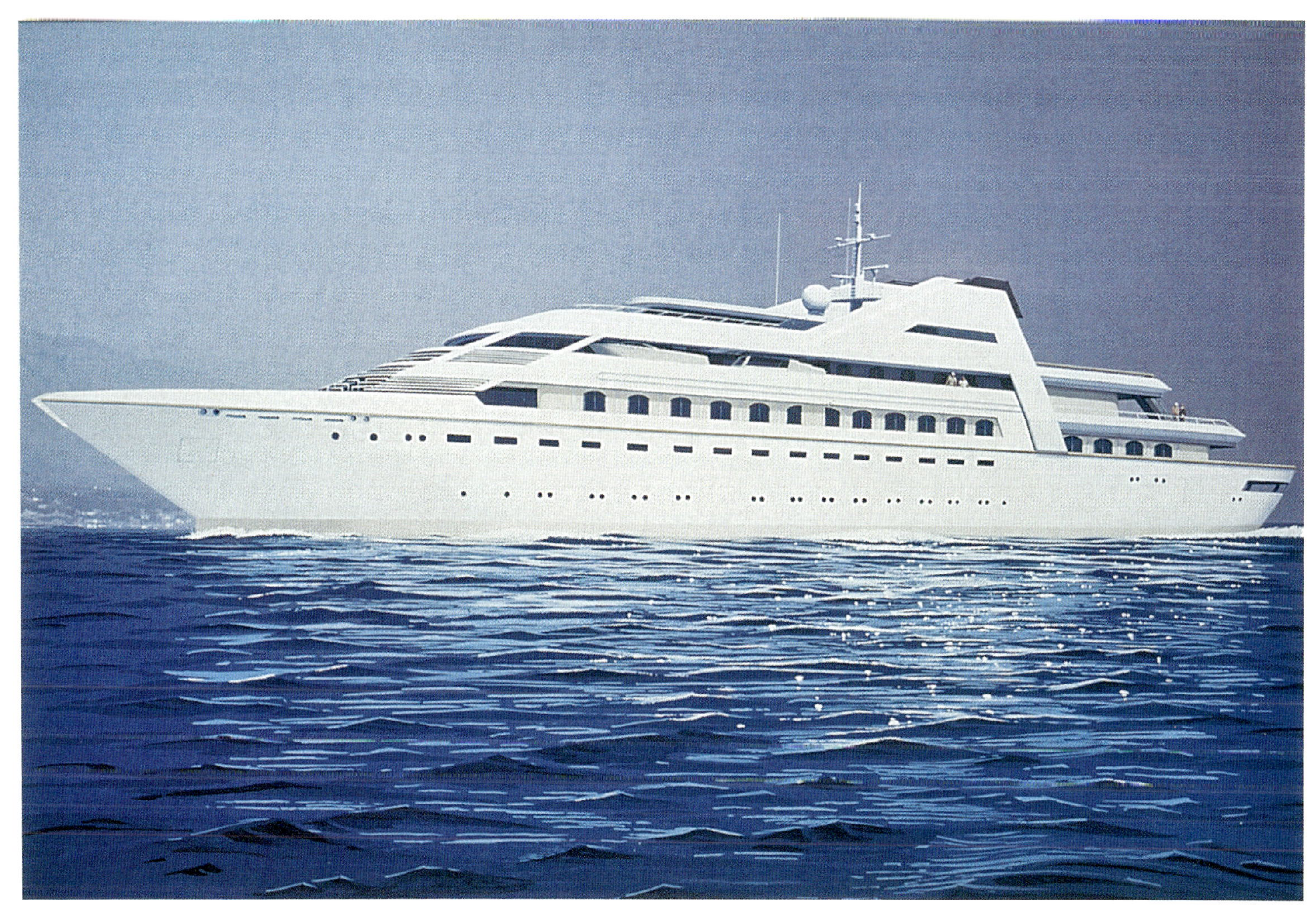

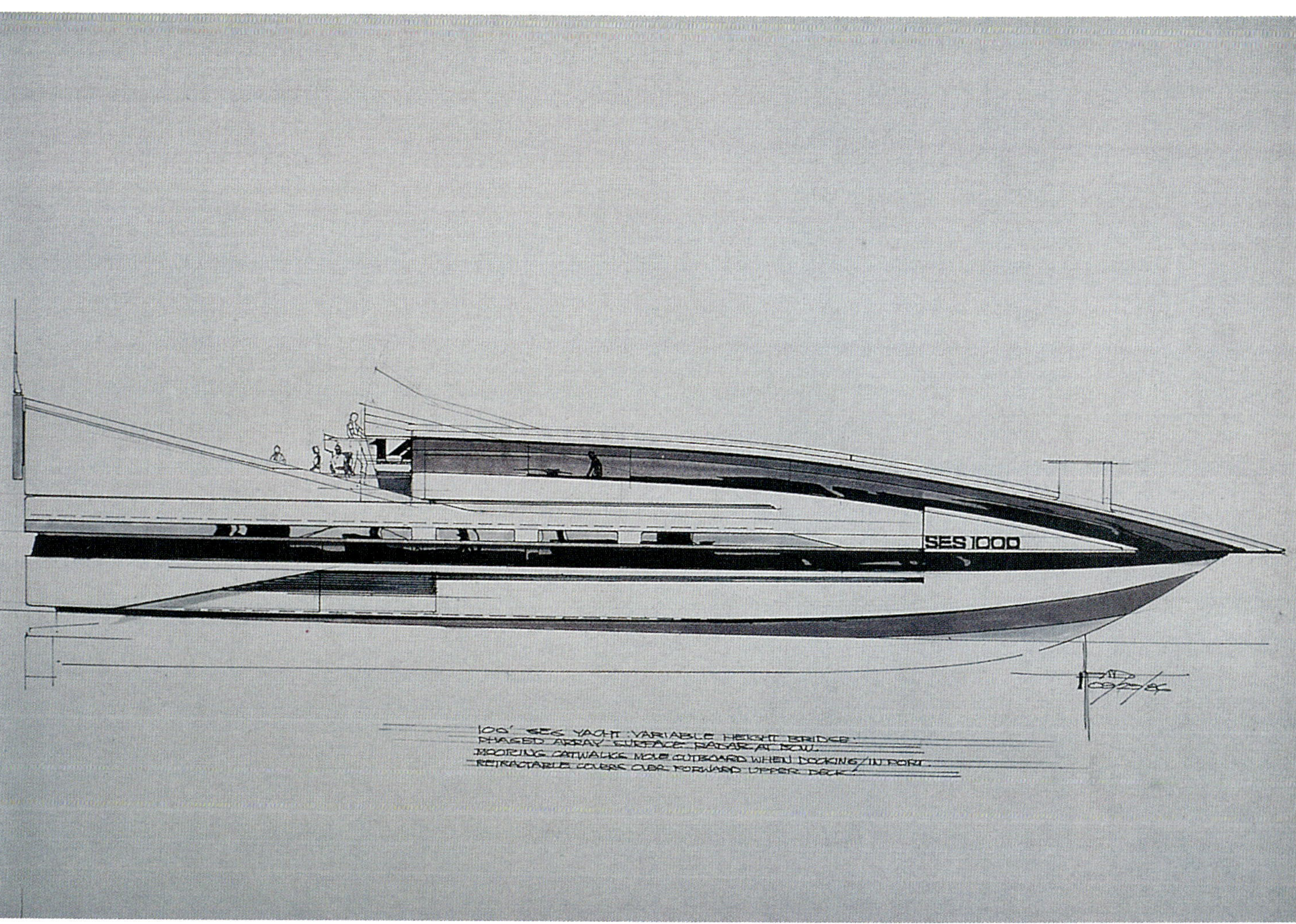

SES 1000
100' SES YACHT: VARIABLE HEIGHT BRIDGE:
PHASED ARRAY SURFACE RADAR AT BOW.
MOORING CATWALKS MOVE OUTBOARD WHEN DOCKING/IN PORT.
RETRACTABLE COVERS OVER FORWARD UPPER DECK.

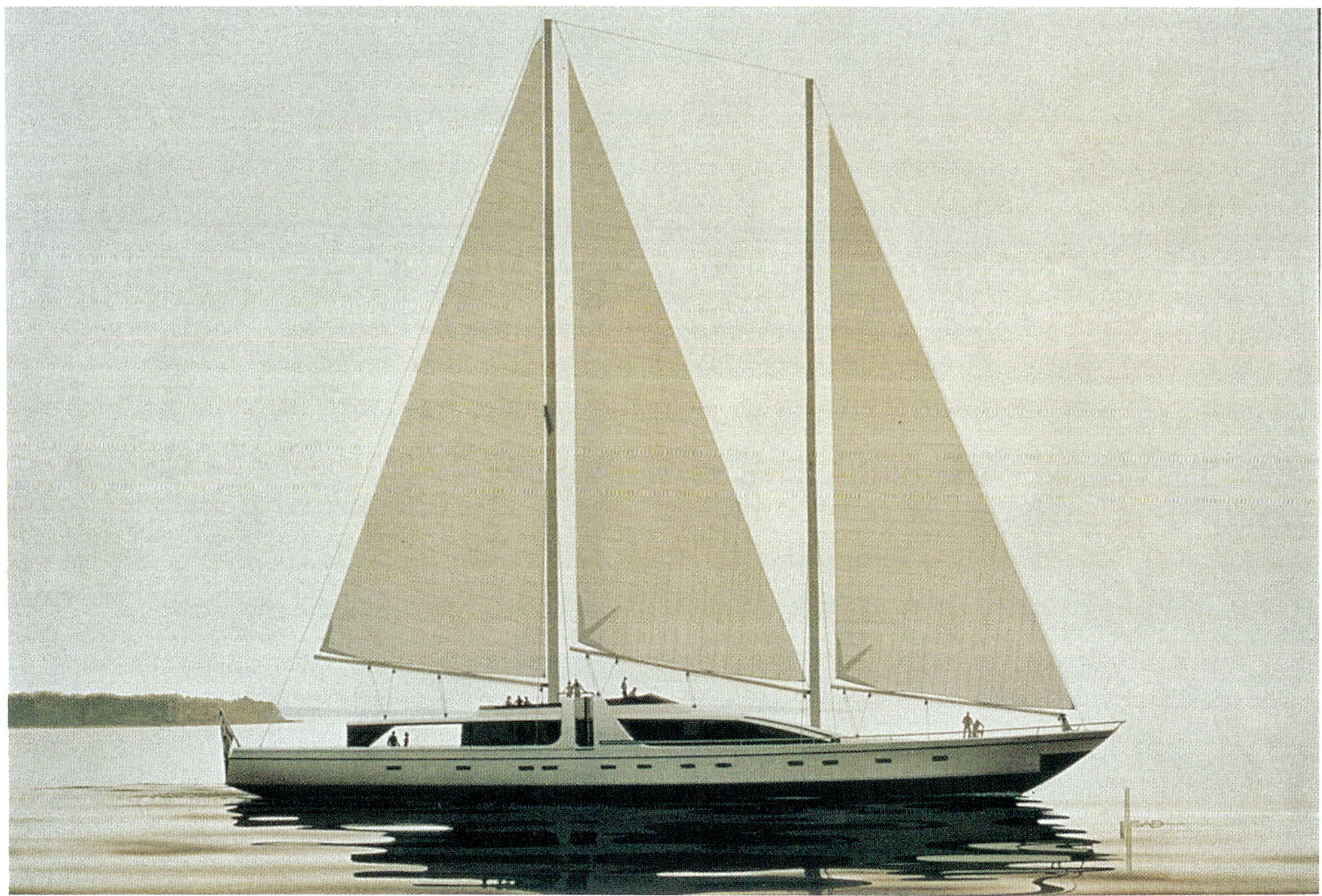

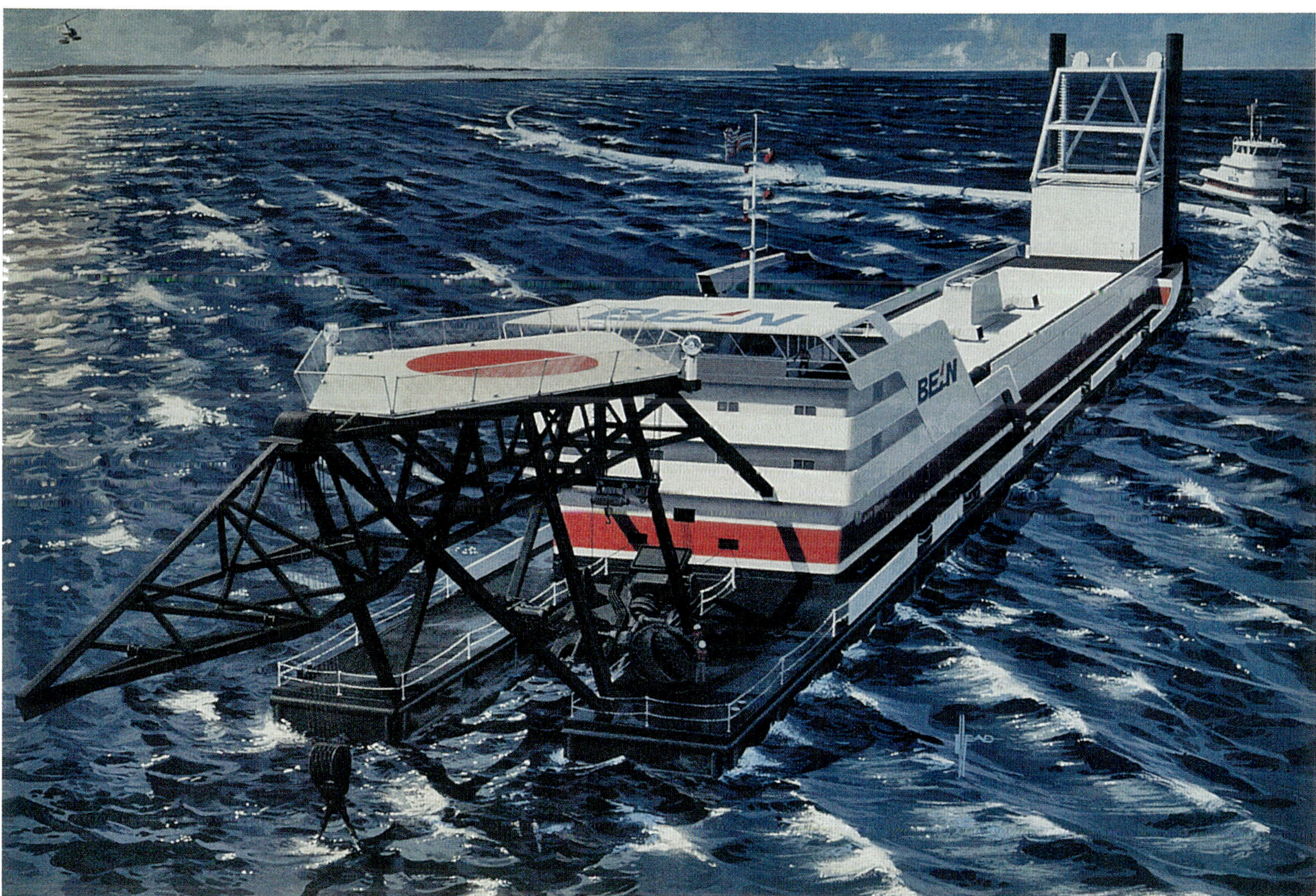

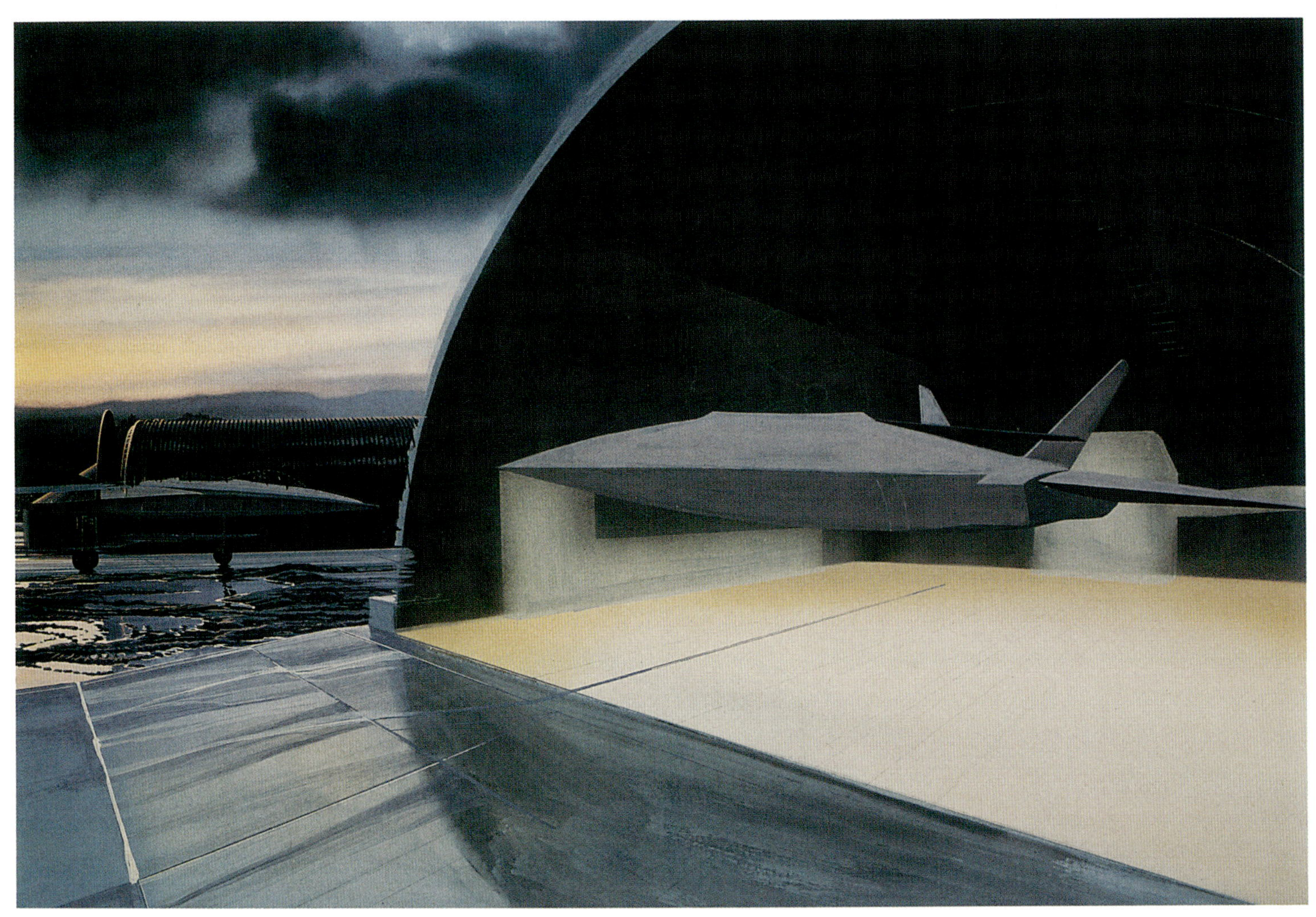
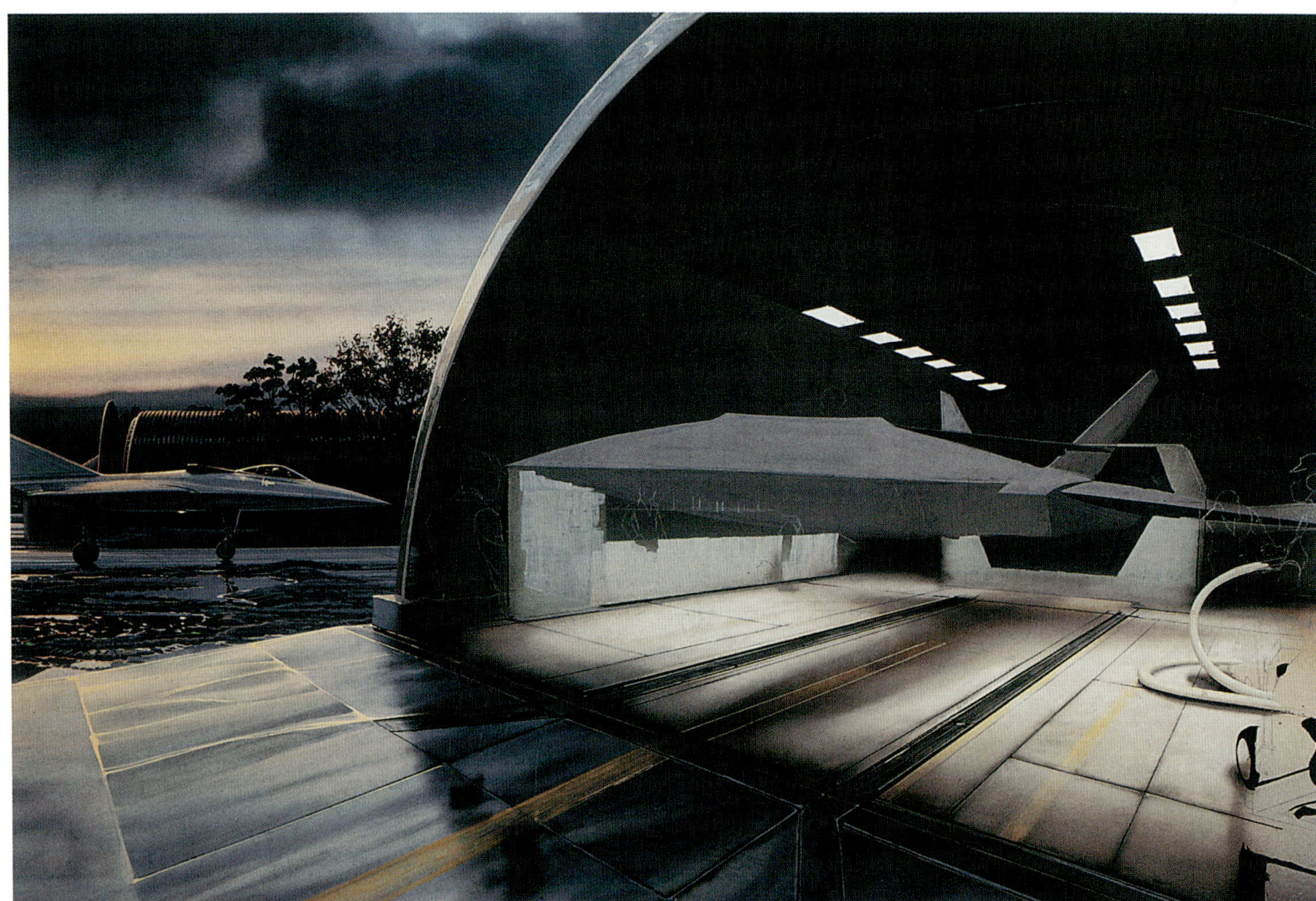
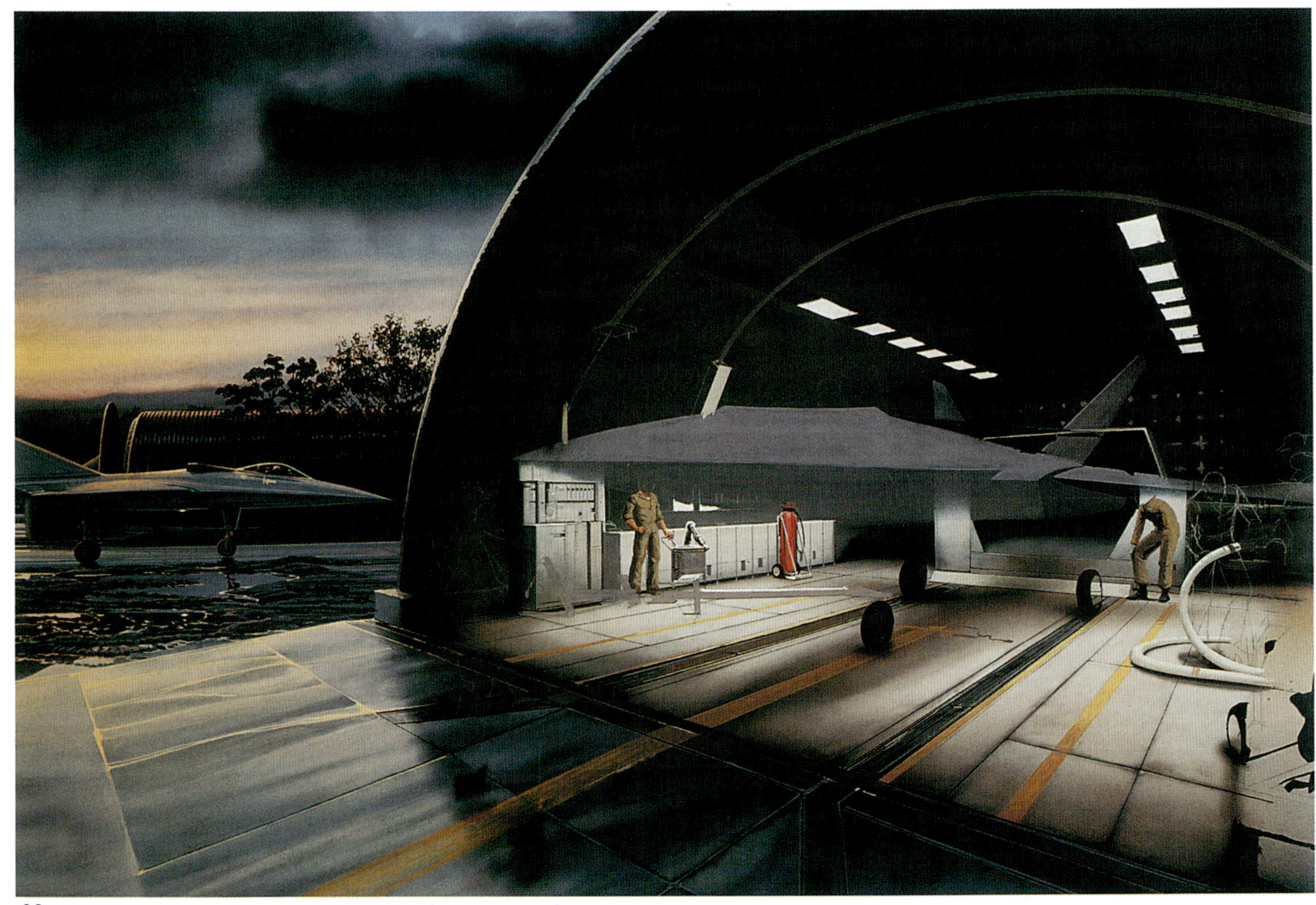
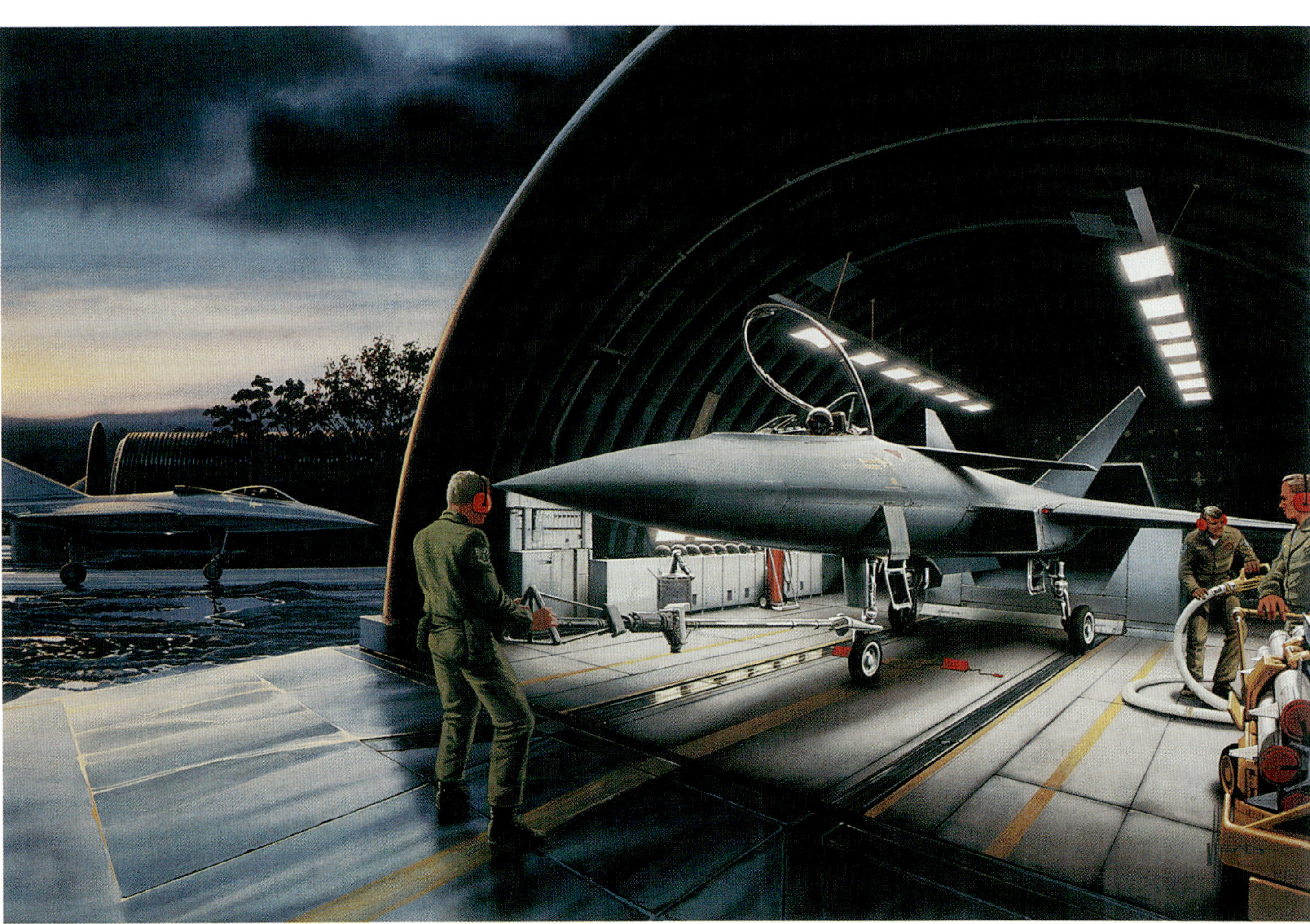

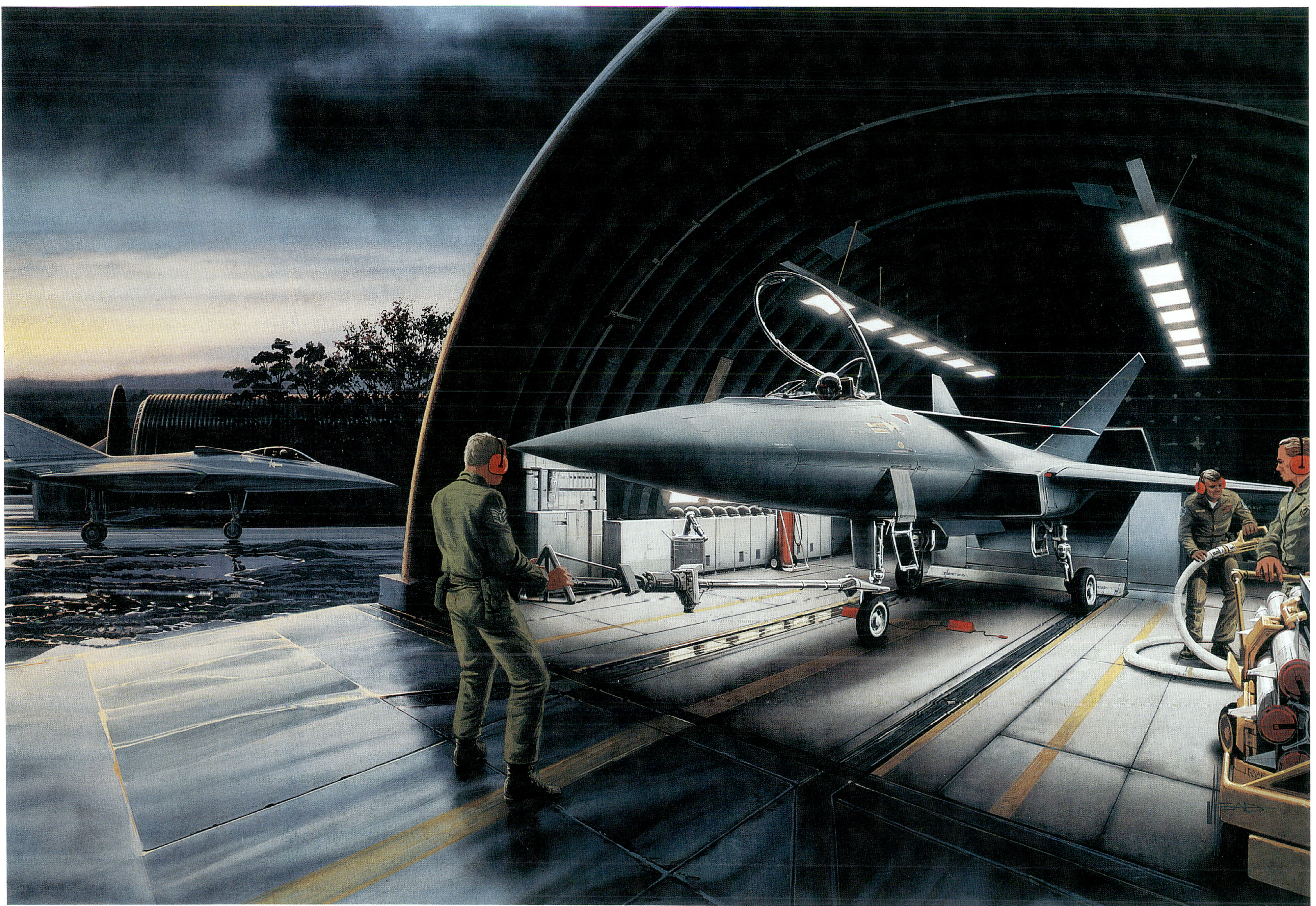

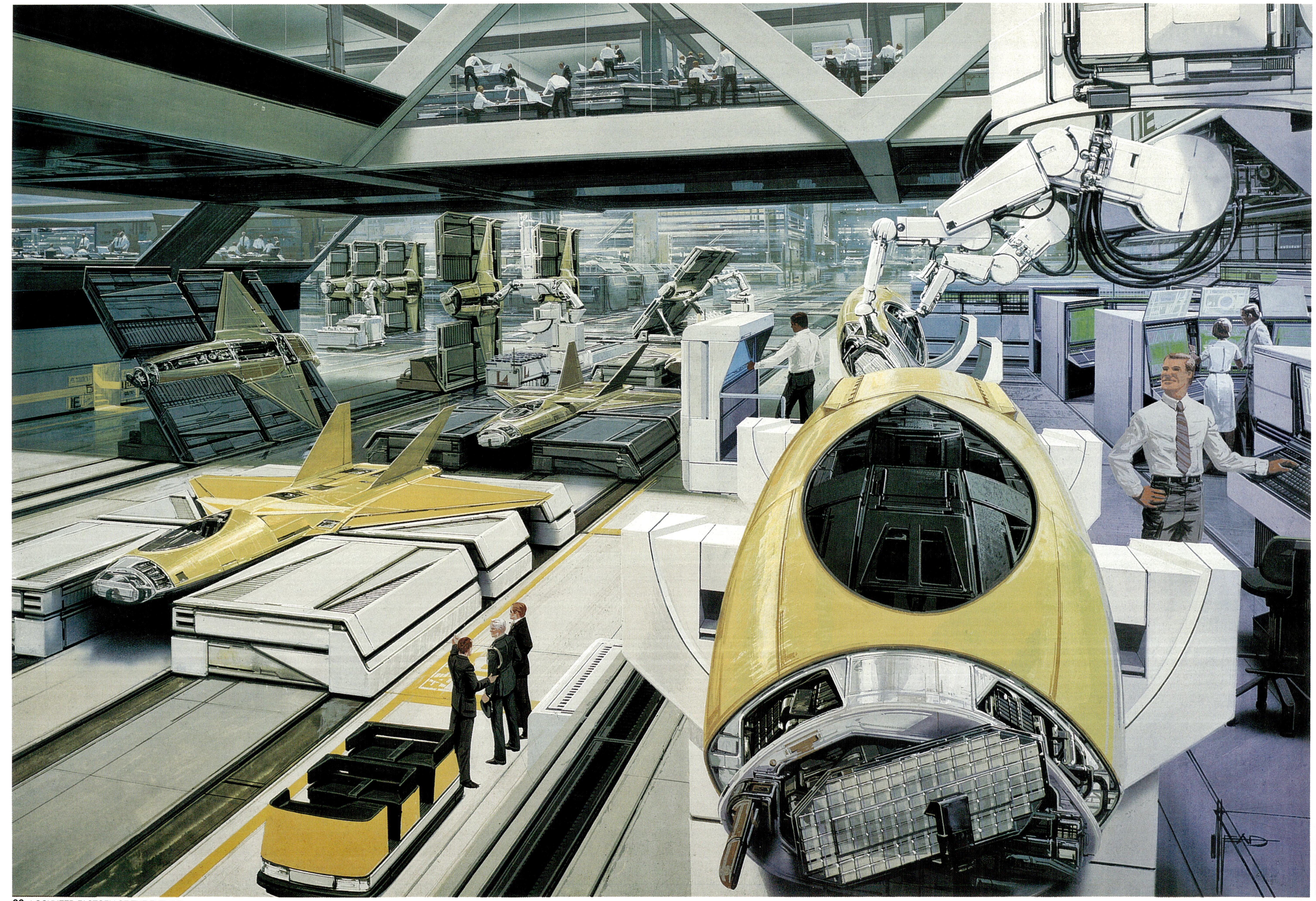

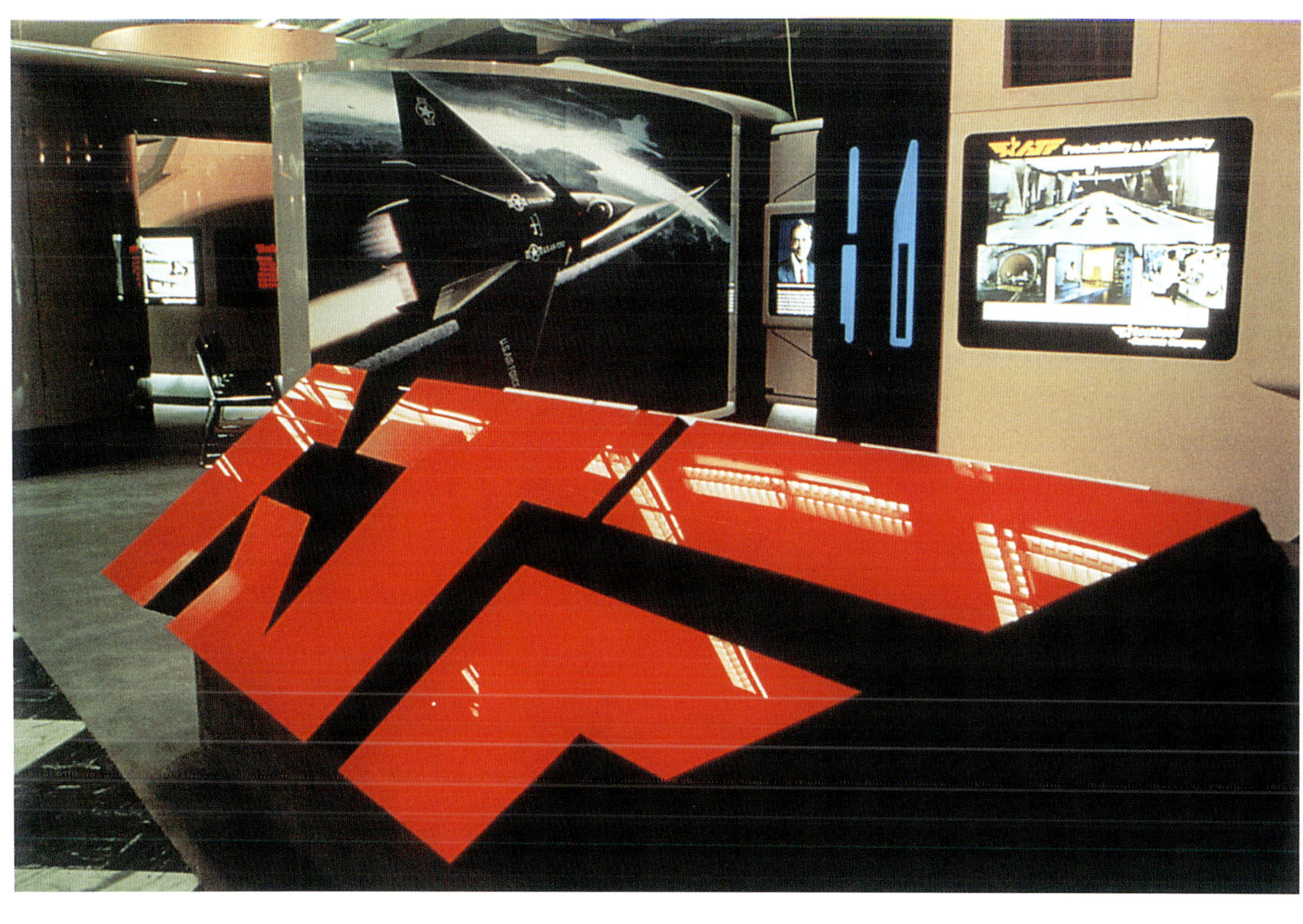

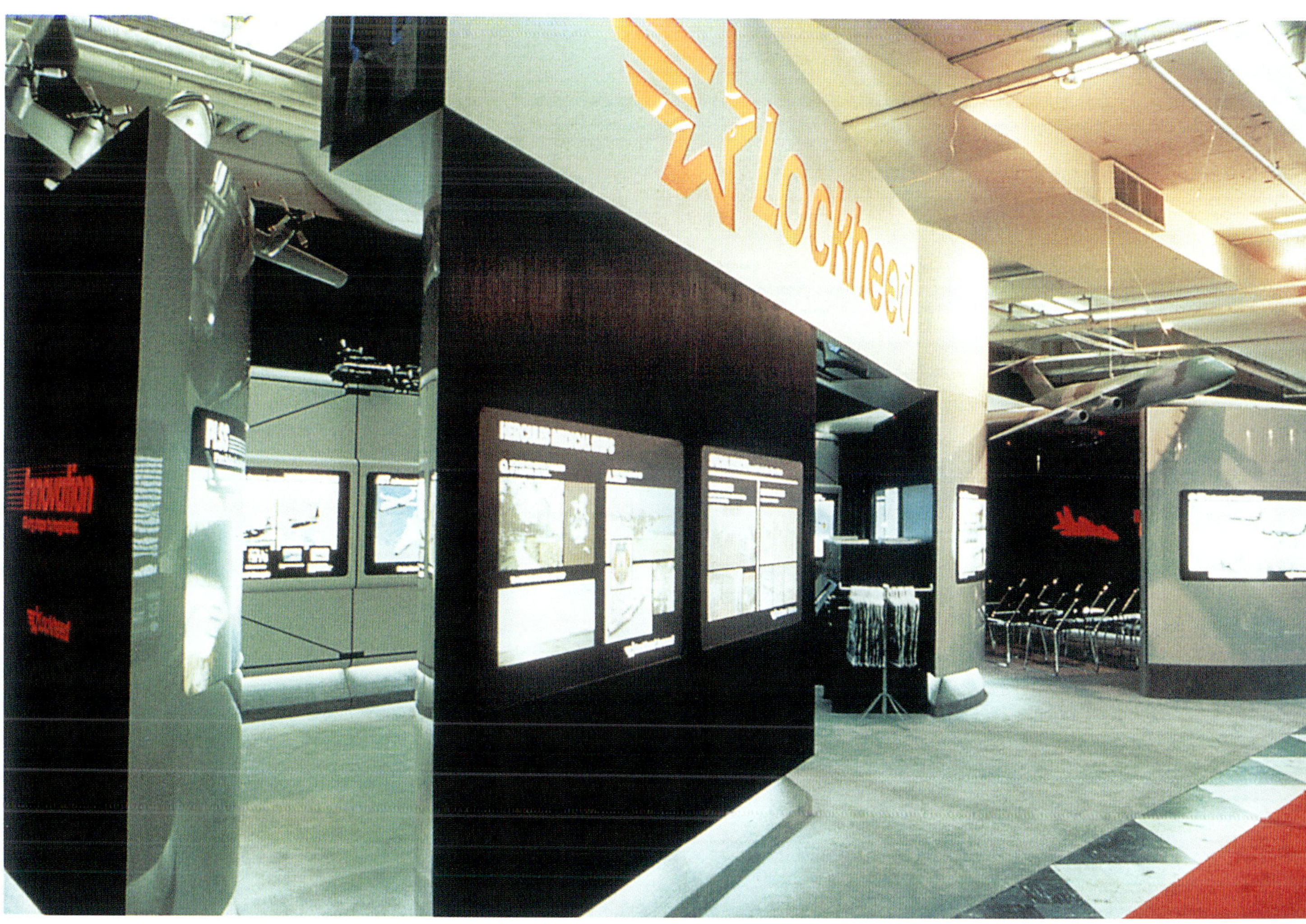

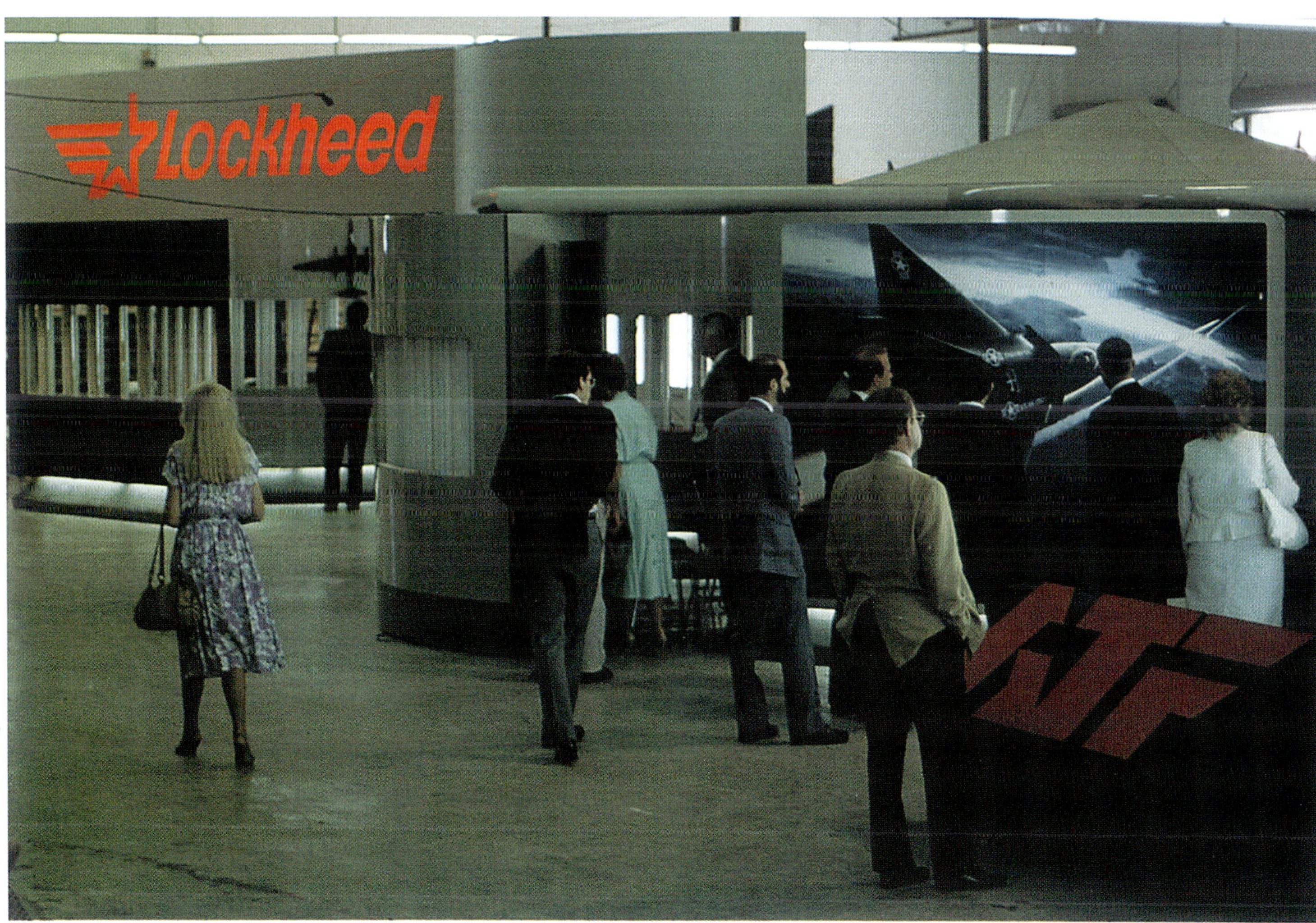

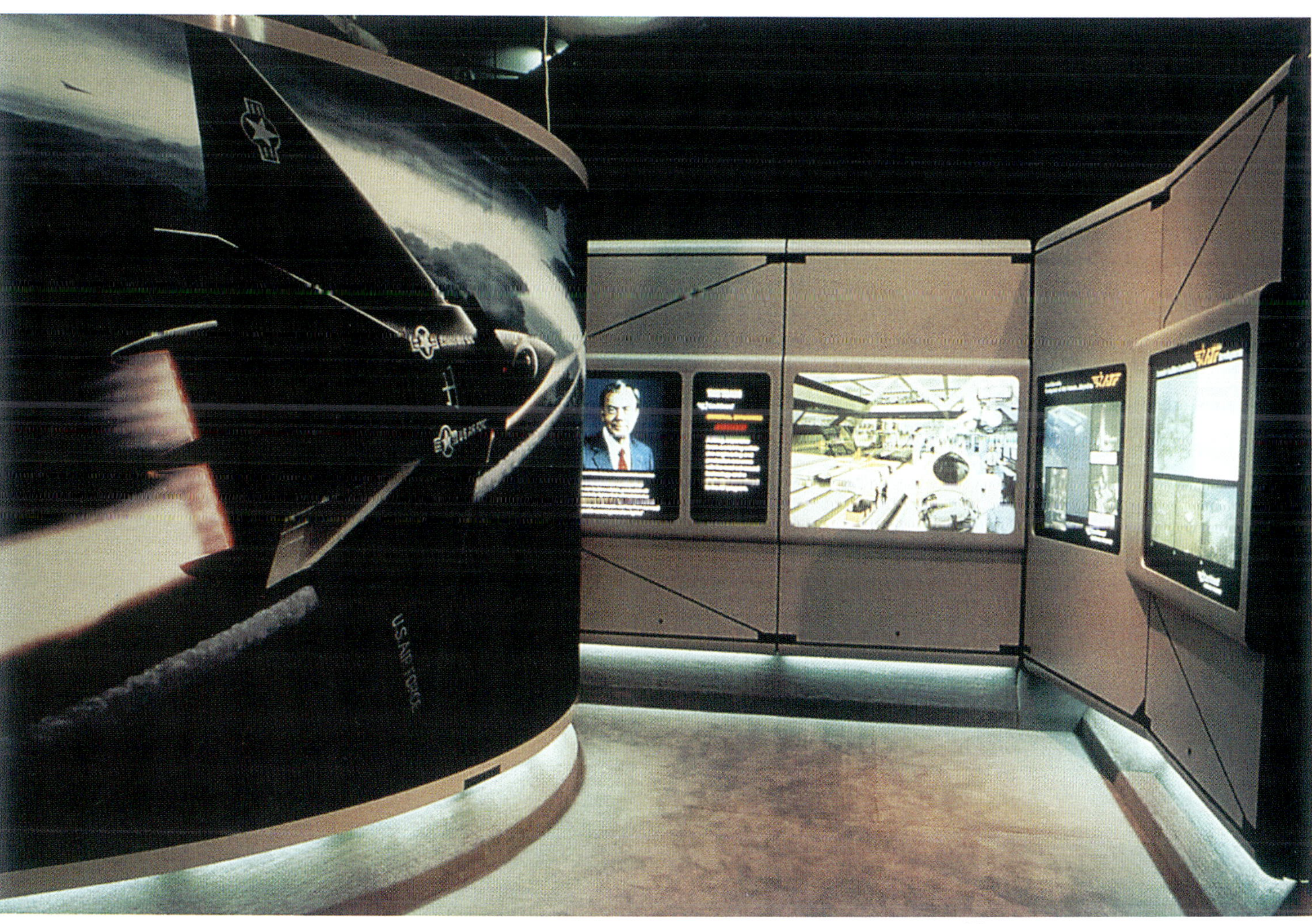

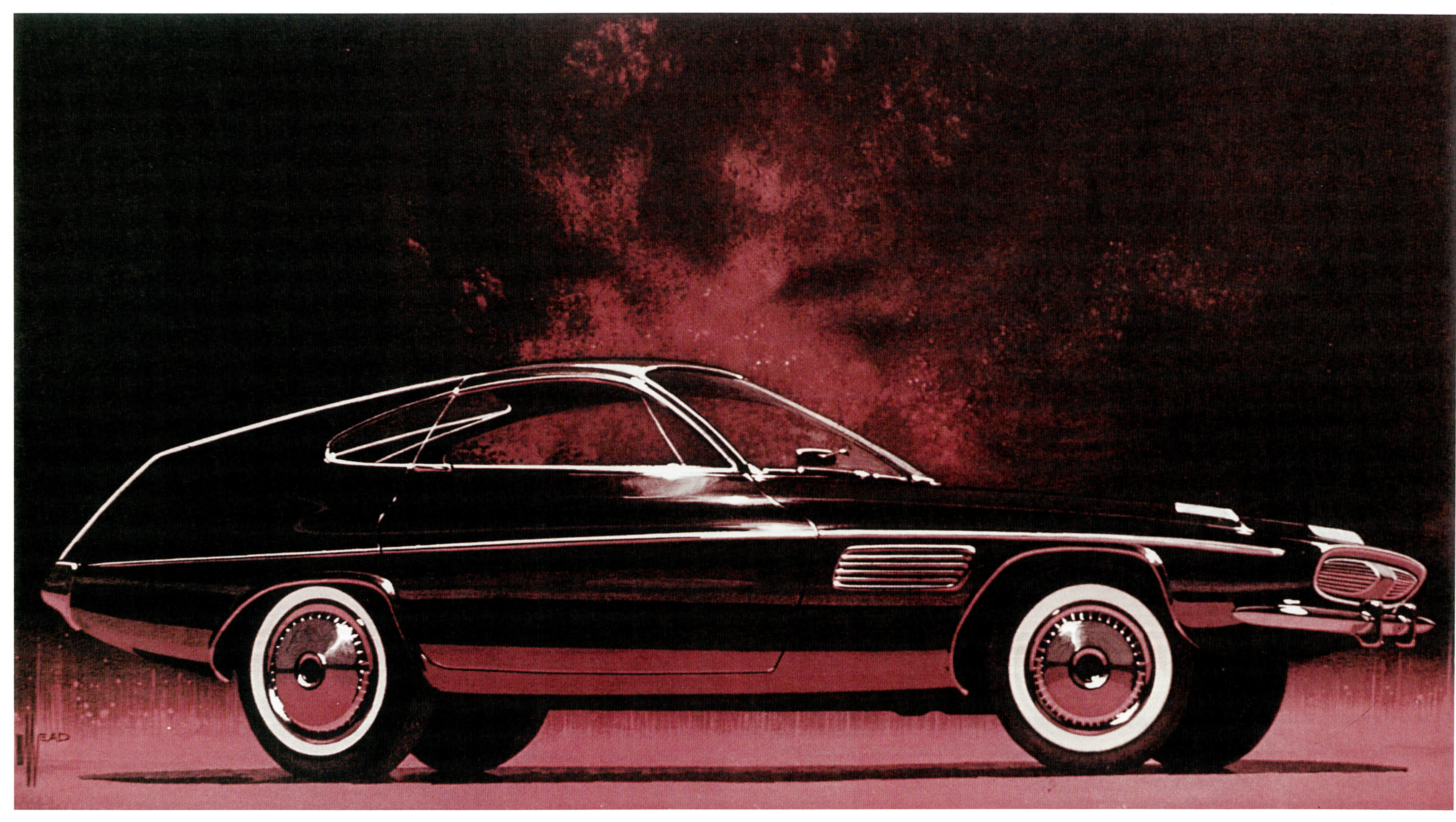

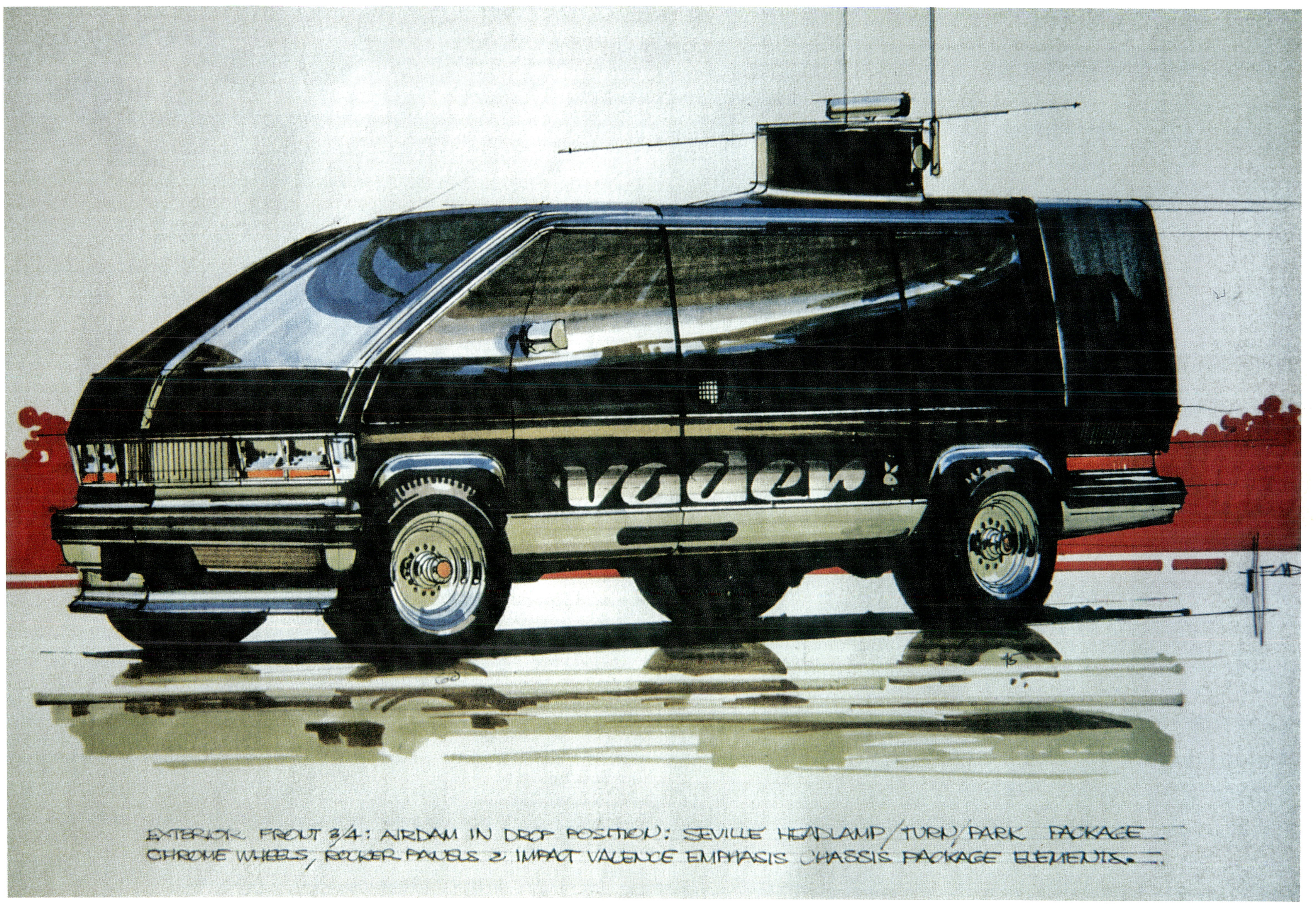

EXTERIOR FRONT 3/4: AIRDAM IN DROP POSITION: SEVILLE HEADLAMP/TURN/PARK PACKAGE
CHROME WHEELS, ROCKER PANELS 2 IMPACT VALENCE EMPHASIS CHASSIS PACKAGE ELEMENTS. T.

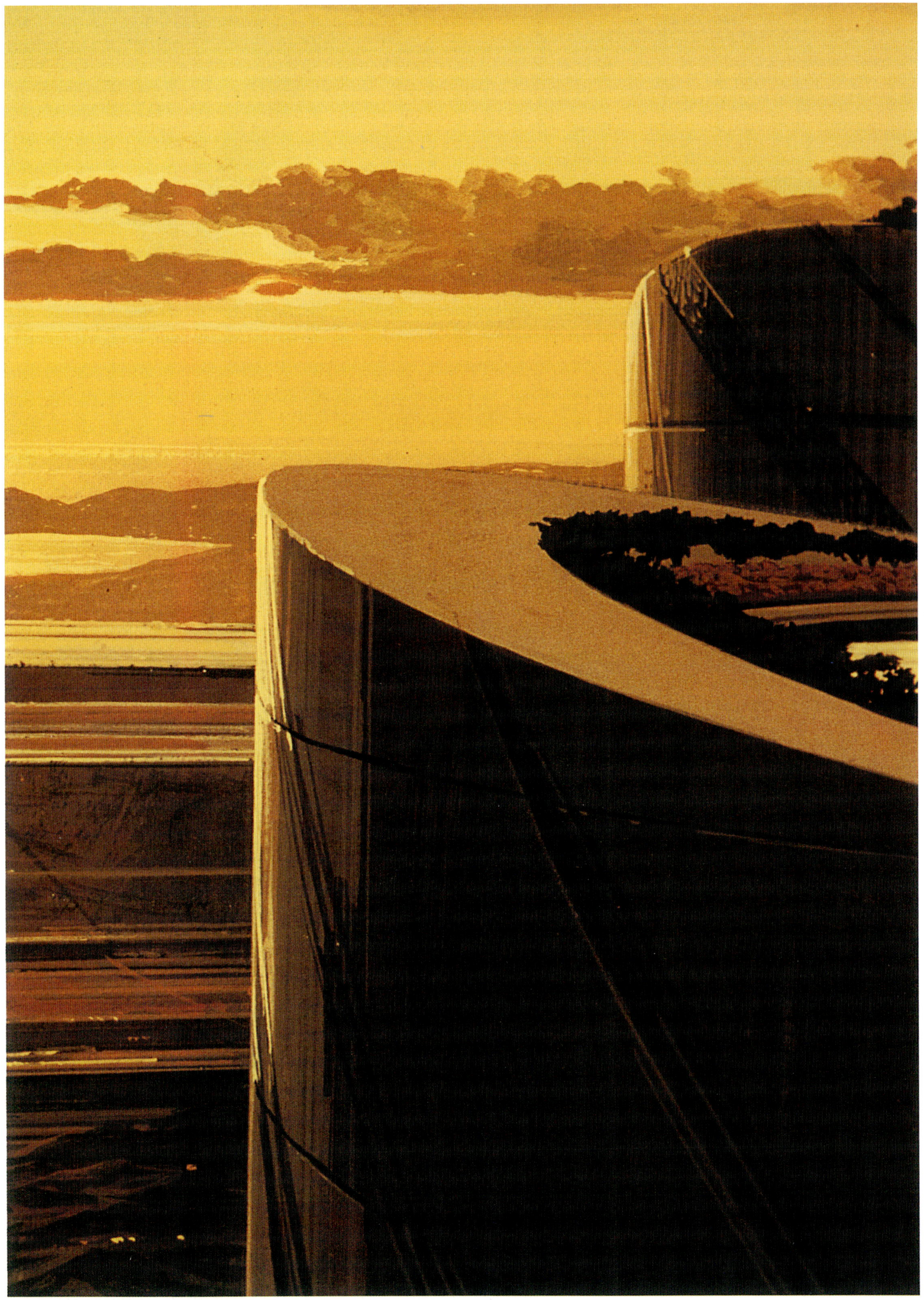

Originally published as

"STUDIO IMAGE TWO"

Published by OBLAGON, INC.
1716 N. Gardner St.,
Los Angeles, CA 90046

FAX: (213) 851-9642
PHONE: (213) 850-5225

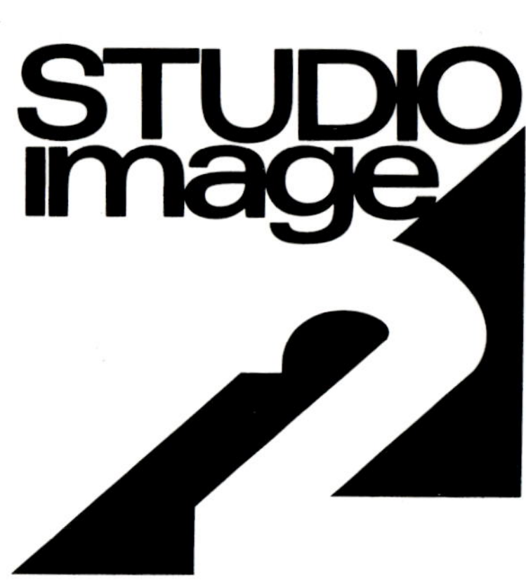

COMMISSIONING ENTITIES FOR THE FOLLOWING WORKS:

2. GENERAL ELECTRIC

3. ALIA, INCORPORATED

4. LOS ANGELES TIMES

5., 8., 13. FORD MOTOR COMPANY

6. GUBER / PETERS

9., 10., 11. NEW REGENCY

12., 34. U.S. STEEL

15. CONRAC

16. SINGER

17. THE BLADE RUNNER PARTNERSHIP, 1982

18., 19. PETER HYAMS PRODUCTIONS, INCORPORATED

21. TIGER

22., 23. NORTHERN TELECOM

24., 28. HALTER YACHTS

27. "SHORT CIRCUIT" TRI-STAR

30., 31., 32., 33. LOCKHEED

35. PLAYBOY

36. SPROCKET, INCORPORATED

PRODUCTION CREDIT

All Illustrations: Syd Mead

Art Direction: Tim Bradley

Layout Design: Syd Mead, Inc.

Printing: Columbia Lithograph, Inc.

© OBLAGON, INC. 1989

Rev. 3/96

Published August 1989

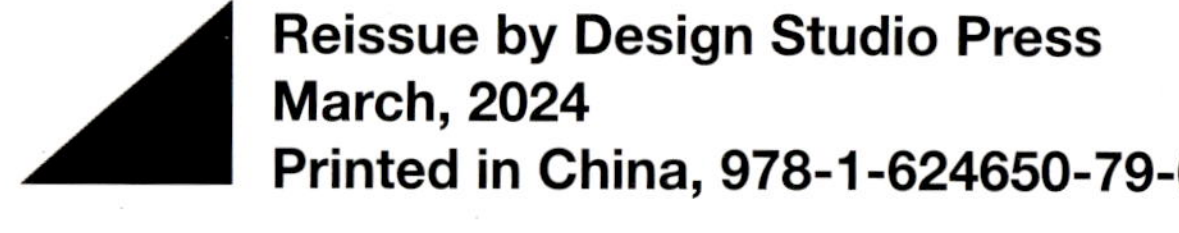
**Reissue by Design Studio Press
March, 2024
Printed in China, 978-1-624650-79-6**